SYMBOLIZATION

Representation and Communication

Editor

James Rose

Series Editors

Inge Wise and *Paul Williams*

KARNAC

First published in 2007 by the Institute of Psychoanalysis, London

British Library Cataloguing in Publication Data

A C.I.P. for this book is available from the British Library

ISBN 978 1 85575 590 1

Designed, typeset, and produced by The Studio Publishing Services Ltd,
www.studiopublishingservicesuk.co.uk
e-mail: studio@publishingservicesuk.co.uk

Printed in Great Britain

10 9 8 7 6 5 4 3 2 1

www.karnacbooks.com

CONTENTS

ACKNOWLEDGEMENTS

I thank the *International Journal of Psychoanalysis* for permission to reprint the following:

Cavell, M. (1998). Triangulation, one's own mind and objectivity. *International Journal of Psychoanalysis*, *79*: 449–467. © Institute of Psychoanalysis, London, UK.

I am also grateful to Thomson Publishing Services on behalf of Taylor & Francis Books, UK for permission to use "A psychoanalytic approach to perception", from *The Work of Psychic Figurability* (2005), by Cesar and Sara Botella.

Permission to reproduce "A connection between a symbol and a symptom", (Freud, 1916c), is by arrangment with Paterson Marsh Ltd, London.

James Rose, PhD, is a Fellow of the Institute of Psychoanalysis and a member of the British Psychoanalytical Society. He has a private psychoanalytic practice in London. He has worked in the Brandon Centre, an inner city charity specializing in the psychotherapeutic treatment of adolescents and young adults for the past twenty years.

CHAPTER ONE

Symbols: on their formation and use

James Rose

Introduction

B ecause psychoanalysis is a science of subjectivity, it is no
surprise that symbols and symbolic phenomena have been
of central interest from its inception and early development.
There are few phenomena more obviously subjective than symbols.
They conjure a particular fascination because of their enigmatic
quality. For this reason, they manage to communicate something in
an obscure manner. Thus, they partly hide. This duality and ambiguity approaches the fleeting and evanescent quality of subjectivity
itself, at its most subjective. The word *symbol* is derived from the
Greek *symbolon*, which denoted an object cut in two, constituting a
sign of recognition when those who carry it (them) can assemble the
two pieces. It was used by members of the early Christian church
during times of persecution when it could be fatally dangerous to
announce one's faith without ensuring the identity of those to
whom one spoke.

Thinking about symbols in this descriptive way introduces us to
their complexity. However, it is not the most immediately helpful approach to understanding symbols as phenomena, because

it omits immediate consideration of how symbols are formed and how they are used by the individual and the groups that seem to gather around them. The essence of a symbol is that it has a meaning for someone. It is this that distinguishes a symbol from a sign, which is usually taken to mean a stimulus for some kind of action. This action is not necessarily mediated in any way by conscious thought. A danger sign is a prompt to escape the danger without any pause for thoughtful reflection. Pavlov's dogs formed associative links between the ringing of a bell and salivation, which were termed conditioned reflexes. These links, however, did not create symbols because the "symbolizer" had no conscious choice in how to respond on presentation of the sign. Thus, the bell does not become the symbol of meat to the dog.

This simple division between symbol and sign based on the possibility of choice and thought does not quite stand up to the test of experience when we hear a fire alarm. Whether we waste no time to escape the building probably depends on other cues besides the alarm bell itself. The smell of smoke and the sound of running feet and alarmed voices will no doubt influence how we interpret the danger. If we suggest that a sign stands for action whereas a symbol represents an experience, then I think we get to something more useful, particularly if we add that the experience itself may only be partly open to consciousness. It is this that makes the symbol of interest to students of subjectivity.

Initially, the promise of symbols to the pioneers of psychoanalysis was based on their offering access to the unconscious. Like dreams—and manifest in dreams—they seemed to promise to be part of the "royal road to the unconscious".

An example comes from Joan Riviere (1924) who reported in the *International Journal of Psychoanalysis* that:

> Speaking of homo-sexuality between women for the first time in analysis, a woman patient expressed disgust at such a practice. On being asked the origin of this feeling, she said: "Well, it's not so much disgusting, perhaps, as boring. I mean it seems such a pointless idea, so utterly meaningless—like trying to play tennis without balls!" The next moment she herself laughed at the quite unconscious significance of what she had said. [p. 85]

The development of the concept of
symbolism in psychoanalytic theory

Freudian psychoanalysts have differed from their Jungian counterparts in their regard for symbols because they have been increasingly narrowing their focus on to individual experience. The idea that symbols might have some cultural relevance, giving access to a collective unconscious, is of little interest to many of the Freudian persuasion, be they classical Freudian or followers of one of the post-Freudian pioneers. Exceptions might be thought to be the Lacanian development, with its development of the concept of the symbolic order as distinct from the real, and the imaginary orders and the work of Winnicott and associates (e.g., Milner), who have sought to show that artistic endeavour could be understood through the concept of transitional space and transitional phenomena.

In recent years, symbols as phenomena have not captured the imagination of the psychoanalytic community in quite the way they once did. The last symposium at an IPA congress on symbol formation was in 1978, to which Harold Blum and Hanna Segal contributed. At the IPA congress in Chile in 2000 there was a contribution to a panel on "Affect, somatization and symbolization", notably by Joyce McDougall. Why there has been a comparative silence in the literature since is not easy to gauge. It hardly seems that all there was to be said about the symbol had been said. Perhaps it was the Lacanian claim for the symbolic order that had something to do with it. At the symposium in Jerusalem in 1978, Harold Blum stated quite categorically that the unconscious was not structured like a language as if it were an objective fact rather than a way of thinking about the unconscious.

Over the past century, development of the concept of symbolism has taken place within the different meta-psychological frameworks as they have emerged. Jones' paper "On symbolism", written in 1915 as a public lecture, was an effort to emphasize the significance of symbols as providing evidence for clearly unconscious processes. At the time this had an obviously political significance because the Freudian ideas were competing with the Jungian ones. The British Psychoanalytical Society had only just been formed and the establishment of the unconscious as something of scientific interest and a legitimate object of serious scientific research could not be taken for granted. Jones was battling not just for an acceptance of Freud's ideas but also to raise the status of psychoanalysis to one of a science and a method of legitimate psychological inquiry.

However, Jones saw symbols as rather primitive, demonstrating a poverty or deficiency in a capacity to communicate. Nevertheless, he saw them providing evidence for the existence of unconscious process.

If the interest in symbols to psychoanalysts in the early part of the last century was because they provided evidence for unconscious process, the reason for their being of interest had changed by the middle of the century. In this country, the Controversial Discussions (see King & Steiner, 1992), prompted by the arrival of Viennese psychoanalysts into a British Psychoanalytical Society heavily influenced by Melanie Klein, created a tension because the protagonists used different models of subjectivity often without realizing it. At its most fundamental, the issue that divided British psychoanalysis was the philosophical one of how we can know reality in the sense of its objectivity. Freud believed that we can never know reality in a totally objective sense.

Freud (1915) held that:

> In psychoanalysis there is no choice for us but to assert that mental processes are in themselves unconscious, and to liken the perception of them by means of consciousness to the perception of the external world by means of the sense organs.

And further that,

> Just as Kant warned us not to overlook the fact that our perceptions are subjectively conditioned and must not be regarded as identical to what is perceived though unknowable, so psycho-analysis warns us not to equate perceptions by means of consciousness with the unconscious mental processes which are their object. Like the physical, the psychical is not necessarily in reality what it appears to be. [*ibid.*]

If we accept that our perception of reality must be a creation partly determined by unconscious processes and born from our desires, of which we are only partly aware, then we must accept that we cannot fully grasp the external world. This is Freud's radical proposition, which challenged and continues to challenge our illusion that we are essentially rational beings. Klein's concept of "unconscious phantasy" led some to believe that it was possible and technically important to interpret in the transference a patient's hostile impulses towards the analyst. This they did much sooner than a classically trained psychoanalyst, who would wait until it was clear that such hostility was interfering with the free associative process.

As mentioned above, thinking in this descriptive way is not the most immediately helpful approach to understanding symbols as phenomena, because it omits immediate consideration of how symbols are formed and how they are used by the individual and the groups that seem to gather around them. Initially, the promise of symbols to the pioneers of psychoanalysis was based on their offering an access to the unconscious.

As Blum (1978) remarked in his summary of the colloquium on symbol formation at the IPA Congress in Jerusalem in 1976, there has been a tendency to concentrate on what symbols might mean rather what created them in the first place and what their function might be. Thus he said:

> The whole subject of symbolism remains of great importance and a central topic for psychoanalysis, but has received infrequent systematic study (Donadeo, 1974). While there is much in the literature on the meaning of various symbols, there is little theoretical discussion of the symbolic process and symbol formation, and considerations of the different symbolic forms and products. It is now common knowledge, even for the layman that a train can represent a penis and a tunnel, a vagina, but the how and why of symbolism has been relegated to scattered articles in the psychoanalytic literature. [p. 455]

Without fully understanding its implications, most psychoanalysts have used an essentially Cartesian concept of subjectivity (see Cavell, 1998). As Cavell has pointed out, this concept can be characterized as "the first person view". The problem with this position is how one introduces a notion of objectivity. As a beginning in thinking about how different analysts have addressed this problem (often, I think, without quite realizing what they were doing or why they needed to do it), we may say that one group of British analysts adopted an essentially neo-Platonic model. Another sought to resolve this difficulty by adopting a developmental benchmark based on the irreversible process of chronological time reflected by the fact that we all grow up and that children do not have the same cognitive or emotional capacities as adults. That is because they are developing them, and how each individual develops them in part determines their subjective experience as adults. As a result of this bifurcation in direction, it sometimes seems as if one group of British psychoanalysts sought to conquer the unconscious whereas another sought to re-establish it and make it available to be used. When reading Milner and, to a certain extent, Rycroft, one is reminded of the railings of William Blake against "Urizen", otherwise known as Isaac Newton, the apotheosis of the rationalism of the enlightenment.

This creates a dilemma which some solved by insisting on psychoanalysis having solely a subjective focus. Others have found this too solipsistic for their taste, and from this difference flow a host of theoretical and practical consequences that are manifest—to give one example—in questions to do with how we can know what is important about an individual's history in determining their subjective experience. Indeed, this extends to whether, and if so, how, we can know the reality of anyone's history in the sense of it being possible to discover the objective facts. There are those who say that this can only be discovered by the analysis of the transference as revealed in the psychoanalytic setting defined in the consulting room. Immediately, in these debates, one can see an inevitable dialectic between subjective and objective, but with a whole new twist on the notion of the objective brought about by the fact that in psychoanalysis we are dealing with the ideographic: that is, the nature of individual experience.

The confrontation with these scientific, methodological and essentially philosophical issues about subjectivity meant that the idea of symbols having an explanatory relevance beyond the understanding of the individual became increasingly problematical. We can note that the various seminal papers published since the 1950s have a common feature in that they seek to use symbolic phenomena as providing evidence for a particular metapsychological position. If we look at the papers published during the 1950s; e.g., Milner (1952), Rycroft (1956), Segal (1957), and Winnicott (1951), we can see a divergence not only of theoretical opinion but also in that of objective. It is as though one group of writers, Klein (1930) and Segal (1957), were seeking to bring primary processes under control whereas others were trying to unfetter them. It is interesting to find both Milner and Segal describing, and using the terms, symbolic equations and symbolic representations, but with a quite different outlook in mind.

Thus, these papers reflect the development of metapsychology in this period and the interesting thing is that they all have something useful to say, both theoretically and practically. The practising psychoanalytic psychotherapist will find something useful in all of them, regardless of the reader's theoretical predilection. However, the possibility that any of these papers provides the crucial or essentially distinguishing clue to resolving philosophical issues to do with subjectivity and objectivity and their relationship still seems to elude us.

This probably should be unsurprising. If the unconscious does not give up its secrets easily, we can be sure that metaphysical questions and their metapsychological counterparts will prove equally redoubtable. What makes the study of symbolism and its history interesting is that symbols provide clues to understanding what is obscure—such as a symptom—and the manner of their formation and usage can tell us something important about how and why we can—or fail to—communicate with one another. But, we can go beyond that, in so far as the study of the formation of a symbol can provide a line of approach to the question of how we create our subjectivity. Put in other words, how we create a sense of ourselves and its attendant sense of reality. When applied to the study of an individual's subjective experience, the unique property of the psychoanalytic setting permits the possibility of observing over a period of time how that individual creates his or her sense of the world and the people in it. We see it in the relationship with the psychoanalyst as it gathers and develops in the transference.

This is supposed to be a short book that provides a way into the understanding of the issues I have referred to above. The reader will have already realized that many issues are raised by a study of symbolism. Like the study of language, it is impossible to conduct this study outside the context of its expression. As Chomsky has suggested, the study of signifiers outside their context does not reveal much. For this reason, he did not consider that de Saussure had much of interest to say about linguistics—a position perhaps astonishing to some. A short book cannot be a thoroughly exhaustive text covering all the essential matters in all their aspects. This book is therefore assembled in such a way that the reader can trace the development of the understanding of symbols and their formation and use in its historical context, and to try to look at their clinical significance. This is in the hope that the book will be of relevance and use in the practical sense as well as the theoretical.

To do this, I found it useful to think about two issues. The first concerned what might force an individual subject to use symbols as means of communication. I became interested in the possibility that symbols are developed as part of the means of managing the inevitable and unavoidable anxiety of change. Change—or its prospect—is itself equally unavoidable because we cannot know the future. Thus, I have looked at the development of symbols as a means of communication through the *use of the setting*. This permitted a development of the concept of triangulation referred to by Marcia Cavell (1998), which is reprinted in full in this volume. The basic idea of this concept is that we can only know our own minds through discourse with another mind about something external to both those minds.

As a theoretical concept, triangulation as described by Cavell is an invaluable means of bringing together the subjective with the objective. The only drawback to its full application to the clinical setting is, to my mind, the absence of a temporal dimension. By adding a temporal dimension, we can postulate the idea of progressive triangulation because the essence of the psychoanalytic treatment is that its iterative nature allows a repeated examination of an analysand's experience that progressively deepens and broadens its understanding. This concept is, I think, central to contemporary thinking about symbolization because it suggests a conceptual link with the concept of representation.

Once this is added, then we can develop a conceptual device to handle the emergence of what begins in an analysis as unrepresentable to the patient. Very probably, it is the effect of what it is that is unrepresentable that drives the patient to undergo the rigours of a full psychoanalysis, because these effects can be tormenting. Hence, the second issue concerned thinking about experience that is initially *unrepresentable* in order to observe how that experience becomes represented in the psychoanalytic setting.

In recent years, the importance of representing the unrepresentable has been emphasized by the work of Cesar and Sara Botella. In their book, *The Work of Psychic Figurability* (2005), they arguably make the biggest advance in the understanding of symbolic processes that has been made since the work in the mid-1950s of Winnicott, Milner, and Segal. What is remarkable is that they seek to resuscitate the concept of *darstellbarkeit*, translated as "figurability", which is one of the four functions of the dream work set out in Freud's *The Interpretation of Dreams* (1900a). Unlike condensation, displacement, and secondary revision, figurability seems to have been largely forgotten; possibly because of the difficulty of translating *darstellbarkeit* into English or French. Essentially, they suggest that the representation of experience that has been unrepresentable is a crucially important function of a psychoanalytic treatment. This enables the incorporation of much work with autistic children pioneered by the work of Tustin and Alvarez. Much of the Botellas' clinical material—although not all—is from work with children. A way of conceptualizing these ideas into a kind of category is to suggest that they all emphasize that psychoanalytic work is directed at enabling the analysand to develop representations of unrepresentable experience.

Before I had encountered the Botellas' book, I had been seeking to develop my understanding of Cavell's proposition that we come to know our own minds as a result of a discourse with another mind about something in the external world. To apply this idea to the understanding of subjective experience, I wondered what might emerge if this something was thought of as being nothing. The particular experience I chose was a sense of nothingness, because it is by definition both subjective and unrepresentable. In particular, I had been interested in problems arising from an individual's experience of absence and being a nothing—or nothingness—resulting from decathexis.

Nothingness as a subjective experience was closely linked in my mind with the experience of decathexis as it has been explored by the work of Donnet and Green. Decathexis by a primary object like a mother, in Green's view (1986), creates holes in experience. It seemed to me that it is possible to observe that these holes are then filled with what I have chosen to call *virtual objects*, which are representations of the subject's understanding of the reason for their being decathected. These virtual objects then become observable in the transference and, as such, are indisputably subjective phenomena created in reaction to the experience of being decathected. In a sense, therefore, they become symbolic phenomena, because they represent a means for the patient to communicate to the psychoanalyst something centrally important to the understanding of their difficulties, which have brought them to treatment. This communication is by no means a consciously deliberate one. However, the nature of the psychoanalytic setting is uniquely suited to enable a patient to make these communications unconsciously by means of enactments in the transference.

At another level, the advantage of developing the notion of *progressive triangulation* is that it provides an important rationale for the structure and function of the psychoanalytic setting. Essentially, we create a learning system in which the patient and his unconscious meets the psychoanalyst and her unconscious and a communication can take place. Learning takes place through the work of progressive triangulation. The communication concerns something centrally significant in structuring the analysand's mind and his relationships with others. This something, which is both unconscious and potentially disturbing to the analysand, is not clearly represented in the analysand's mind and is not easily representable to other minds. Psychoanalysis essentially has its effect by repetitively and progressively working through a series of triangulations until there is an understanding of the transference and countertransference issues that is convincing to both patient and his psychoanalyst. Once this is achieved, then the analysis can terminate satisfactorily.

A symbol can thus be defined as a creation by the analysand whose purpose is to represent an experience for an individual and communicate it to another person; possibly, but not exclusively, a psychoanalyst. A symbol, therefore, has a representative and communicative function. The psychoanalytic setting is uniquely suitable for observing the creation of symbols and for developing an understanding of what it is that they seek to communicate.

Symbols come in many forms, but the iterative nature of the psychoanalytic process allows the parties concerned to experience the repetitions of process and thus gradually bring the meaning of the symbol into focus.

This book is structured in the following way. We begin with a very short statement by Freud (1916c) on "A connection between a symbol and a symptom". He proposes the analysis of dreams has "sufficiently well established that the hat is a symbol of the genital organ, most frequently of the male organ". He then observes how an obsessional neurotic can cause themselves continual torments, by being constantly on the look-out to see whether acquaintances will greet them by first doffing their hats or whether they seem to be waiting for him to doff his hat first. He suggests that this reveals the troubling impact of castration anxiety on the obsessional neurotic and how it reveals itself in their beliefs and behaviour in the social world—otherwise known as symptoms. We can see how close symbols and symptoms come to one another, so that it can be said that symptoms function as symbols.

One can take this example to be one that demonstrates in which the individual reveals his neurotic anxieties in his unwitting use of the social situation in his dealings with another person. In so far as this demonstrates a structure of triangulation, it is a good place to begin. We have to bear in mind that without the psychoanalytic setting we will not learn about the castration anxiety, because the purpose of hiding it in the anxiety about the hat doffing is precisely so that the neurotic remains unconscious of his fears, and possibly wishes, concerning castration.

In Chapter Two, we present a reproduction of Marcia Cavell's (1998) paper, "Triangulation: one's own mind and objectivity". This sets out a conceptual framework for thinking about subjectivity and objectivity, which, to my mind, has been essential to thinking objectively about a symbol as a subjective phenomenon. This then creates a framework for thinking about a symbol as a means of communicating anxiety about change, which is the subject of my own chapter that follows Cavell's. The purpose of this chapter is to introduce the notion of progressive triangulation as it is expressed in the iterative learning process that is the basis of the psychoanalytic method.

Having considered symbolization in its communicational aspect, we can then turn to its representational sense. We begin with an extract from the Botellas' book (2005) referred to above, which sets out a psychoanalytic approach to perception. In this extract, they address the apparent paradox of unconscious representation—in other words, how can this be?

They draw attention to Freud's investigations into fetishism (1927e) which

> would offer him the possibility of really approaching the connection between the ego and reality and of coming to terms with the complexity of the role of perception. By constituting a fetishistic object, the fetishist acknowledges in his own way the missing penis in a woman and thus accords sense perception its full importance; but, at the same time, he retains in his endopsychic perception, something irrepresentable and terrifying from his infantile sexuality, the anti-traumatic outcome of which is the belief that women do have a penis. [Botella & Botella, 2005, p. 162]

In so far as such a belief is a negative hallucination, we can begin to see how perception is influenced by unconscious process and hence we can start to see how representation can be unconscious. In their reference to "endopsychic perception" above, men can perhaps imaginatively grasp just what the experience is that is "not felt" because castration is not "seen".

We can also begin to imagine how powerful experiences of the presence and absence of objects can start to be represented—some might say symbolized—in the transference, but in such a way that they are not understood as such by either analyst or analysand. It is this phenomenon that is the subject of the final two chapters, which seek, first, to demonstrate the creation of virtual objects in response to absence of significant others, and, second, to observe the work of the progressive triangulation of psychoanalytic process in revealing the meaning of these unconsciously determined phenomena.

References

Blum, H. (1978). Symbolic processes and symbol formation. *International Journal of Psychoanalysis, 59*: 455–471.

Botella, C., & Botella, S. (2005). *The Work of Psychic Figurability*. Hove: Brunner-Routledge.

Cavell, M. (1998). Triangulation, one's own mind and objectivity. *International Journal of Psychoanalysis, 79*: 449–467.

Freud, S. (1900a). *The Interpretation of Dreams. S.E., 4–5.* London: Hogarth.

Freud, S. (1916c). A connection between a symbol and a symptom. *S.E., 14*: 339–340. London: Hogarth.

Freud, S. (1927e). Fetishism. *S.E., 21*: 147–158. London: Hogarth.

Green, A. (1986). The dead mother. In: *On Private Madness*. London: Hogarth.

King, P., & Steiner, R. (Eds.) (1992). *The Freud–Klein Controversies (1941–1945)*. London: Tavistock.

Klein, M. (1930). The importance of symbol-formation in the development of the ego. *International Journal of Psychoanalysis, 11*: 24–39.

Milner, M. (1952). Aspects of symbolism in comprehension of the not-self. *International Journal of Psychoanalysis, 33*: 181–194.

Riviere, J. (1924). Phallic symbolism. *International Journal of Psychoanalysis, 5*: 85.

Rycroft, C. J. (1956). Symbolism and its relationship to the primary and secondary processes. *International Journal of Psychoanalysis, 37*: 137–146.

Segal, H. (1957). Notes on symbol formation. *International Journal of Psychoanalysis, 38*: j391–397.

Winnicott, D. W. (1951). Transitional objects and transitional phenomena. In: *From Paediatrics to Psychoanalysis*. London: Hogarth, 1982.

CHAPTER TWO

A connection between a symbol and a symptom[1]

Sigmund Freud

Editor's introduction

In this shorter writing by Freud (1916c), he begins by stating
that: "Experience in the analysis of dreams has sufficiently well
established the hat as a symbol of the genital organ, most
frequently of the male organ. It cannot be said that the symbol is an
intelligible one." My point in including it is to illustrate how Freud
saw that links could be made between symptoms—in this paper he
discusses the tortures to which certain obsessional patients subject
themselves—and the symbols, or representations, that they employ
to communicate these agonies to their psychoanalyst. It will be clear
that these communications will not be intelligible to the psychoanalyst unless they understand the equation of doffing a hat with
submission—or castration.

In this very short paper, Freud immediately expands the notion
of a symbol from being an intrapsychic representation to having the
capacity for an interpsychic communication.

* * *

Experience in the analysis of dreams has sufficiently well established the hat as a symbol of the genital organ, most frequently of

the male organ.[2] It cannot be said, however, that the symbol is an intelligible one. In phantasies and in numerous symptoms the head too appears as a symbol of the male genitals, or, if one prefers to put it so, as something standing for them. It will sometimes have been noticed that patients suffering from obsessions express an amount of abhorrence of and indignation against punishment by beheading far greater than they do in the case of any other form of death; and in such cases the analyst may be led to explain to them that they are treating being beheaded as a substitute for being castrated. Instances have often been analysed and published of dreams dreamt by young people or reported as having occurred in youth, which concerned the subject of castration, and in which a round ball was mentioned which could only be interpreted as the head of the dreamer's father. I was recently able to solve a ceremonial performed by a woman patient before going to sleep, in which she had to lay her small top pillow diamond-wise on the other ones and to rest her head exactly in the long diameter of the diamond-shape. The diamond had the meaning that is familiar to us from drawings on walls (*graffiti*); the head was supposed to represent a male organ.[3]

It may be that the symbolic meaning of the hat is derived from that of the head, in so far as a hat can be regarded as a prolonged, though detachable head. In this connection I am reminded of a symptom by means of which obsessional neurotics succeed in causing themselves continual torments. When they are in the street they are constantly on the look-out to see whether some acquaintance will greet them first by taking off his hat, or whether he seems to be waiting for *their* salutation; and they give up a number of their acquaintances after discovering that they no longer greet them or do not return their own salutation properly. There is no end to their difficulties in this connection; they find them everywhere as their mood and fancy dictate. It makes no difference to their behaviour when we tell them, what they all know already, that a salutation by taking off the hat has the meaning of an abasement before the person saluted—that a Spanish grandee, for example, enjoyed the privilege of remaining covered in the king's presence—and that their own sensitiveness on the subject of greeting therefore means that they are unwilling to show themselves less important than the other person thinks he is. The resistance of their sensitiveness to explanations such as this suggests that a motive less familiar to consciousness is at work; and the source of this excess of feeling might easily be found in its relation to the castration complex.

Notes

1. Eine Beziehung zwischen einem Symbol und einem Symptom. *Int. Z. Psychoanal.*, 4(2) (1916), 111; S.K.S.N., 4 (1918), 198 (1922, 2nd ed.); *G.S.*, 5 (1924), 310; Psychoanalyse der Neurosen (1926), 38; Neurosenlehre und Technik (1931), 21; G.W., 10 (1946), 394. English translation: C.P., 2 (1924): 162. (Tr. D. Bryan.) The present translation is based on the one published in 1924.
2. A hat dream is recorded in Chapter VI (E) of *The Interpretation of Dreams* (1900a), *Standard Edition*, 5: 360–362.
3. This case is related in detail in Lecture XVII of Freud's *Introductory Lectures* (1916–1917).

CHAPTER THREE

Triangulation, one's own mind and objectivity

Marcia Cavell

Editor's introduction

I have included this paper in this book primarily because it sets out a concept of triangulation different from the one commonly encountered in psychoanalytic literature, which is usually closely related to the Oedipal complex. Being a philosopher, Cavell brings a perspective and new rigour to thinking about ideas to do with objectivity and subjectivity. Cavell's triangulation relates to the idea that to know our own mind we must relate to another mind about something. As she shows in this paper, this enables us to bring a notion of objectivity into our understanding of subjectivity—in other words, a sense of our experience as it relates to the world. However, it also permits—indeed assumes—that language is a necessity in communication with other minds as is the existence of a world of external reality about which discourse is concerned.

From this, we can see that subjectivity grows from a sense of the objective real world and not the other way around. I have referred to Cavell's notion of triangulation in some of the other chapters. As a result, I felt it important to reproduce fully the original paper because it offers an important backdrop to thinking about the

representational and communicative—indeed, both the intrapsychic and interpersonal aspects of symbolization.

* * *

Some psychoanalysts now hold that an intersubjective model of the
mind and of the analytic situation renders the ideas of truth, reality,
and objectivity obsolete. Arguing from a position of sympathy with
this model, the author contends that nevertheless both a real,
shared, external world and the concept of such a world are indispensable to propositional thought, and to the capacity to know one's
own thoughts as thoughts, as a subjective perspective on the world.
Without the idea of an objective world with which we are in touch
and which we attempt to be more or less objective about, any
so-called intersubjectivist model collapses into the one-person paradigm. The author traces a certain developmental line in twentieth-
century philosophy that supports an intersubjective view, a line that
shows the place of the normative ideas of truth and falsity, right and
wrong, in the advent of mind; it attempts to disentangle the concept
of truth from an authoritarian view that was implicit in Descartes; it
points out connections, and a difference, between the view of triangulation that it argues for and the views espoused by a number of
psychoanalysts. Some implications of this intersubjectivist position
for psychoanalytic practice are considered; for instance: the interre-
lations between the analyst's third-person knowledge of her patient,
and the patient's developing understanding of himself, and what
the concept of unconscious fantasy presupposes.

    Until recently we conceived the mind as essentially monadic,
containing entirely within itself much of its content as well as the
rudiments of its structure. In recent years, however, a number of
psychoanalysts and philosophers have begun to view the mind as
constituted by an interactive, interpersonal world. (The new dis-
covery that connections in the infant brain are made through the
infant's earliest interplay with responsive adults is a graphic neuro-
logical correlate of this thesis.) We think of the observational stance
as within an intersubjective field (Mitchell, 1988, and hold that
knowledge is achieved through a process of dialogue in which
every person's contribution is necessarily partial. I will refer loosely
to these and kindred beliefs as the intersubjective view of the mind,

aware that in both psychoanalysis and philosophy there are important differences among the view's various proponents.

It is a shift with enormous clinical implications, affecting how we think about resistance (Spezzano, 1993), the unconscious (Stolorow & Atwood, 1992), psychic change (Hoffman, 1983), and, of course, the analytic relationship. The "neutral" analytic observer, situated somehow outside the analyst–analysand pair where he or she has privileged access to the truth, has disappeared; between analyst and patient, we recognize, interpretation goes two ways (Hoffman, 1983).

I think that in general the intersubjectivists are on the right track. All the more reason for protecting their position against some mistaken inferences they themselves occasionally draw that actually undermine it. The following passages from recent psychoanalytic writers, with all of whom I am generally in sympathy, represent the sorts of mistakes I have in mind.

1. "'Reality', as we use the term, refers to something subjective, something felt or sensed, rather than to an external realm of being existing independently of the human subject" (Stolorow & Atwood, 1992, pp. 26–27).
2. The idea of analytic "objectivity", Fogel suggests, is "an intellectual remnant of the one-person psychology paradigm". He continues: "Might reducing the object of analysis to the 'interaction' between patient and analyst not mislead us, if it predisposes us to imagine that there is an objective reality, 'out there' between analyst and patient, that one can be 'objective' about?" (Fogel, Tyson, Greenberg, McLaughlin, & Peyser, 1996, p. 885).
3. "If an observation or measurement could establish a truth, that truth could never become untrue. Yet this happens all the time in science" (Spezzano, 1993, p. 30).

Each of these passages says something important. The first and second insist that the only "reality" we can investigate, know, deceive ourselves about, must be within the realm of someone's potential experience. So Kant said, and on this point few philosophers would disagree. But it does not follow that reality is subjective. On the contrary, in the absence of a distinction between what I "subjectively"—or even we, putting our "subjectivities" together—believe to be the case (a belief which itself is as much a part of reality as the chair I am sitting on), and what is the case, however that is ascertained, the concept of reality loses its sense. In what follows, it will emerge, I hope, that objective reality is a concept indispensable to human affairs.

The third passage warns that *what we take to be a truth* can always be called into question at another time, or under other circumstances; that our claims to truth must always be provisional; that a truth claim is always that, a claim, requiring support; that between the best evidence and *what is the case* there will always be a gap; that a justified belief and a true belief are, unfortunately, not necessarily the same; that talk about "the truth", especially "sincere", self-righteous talk, is often a way of dignifying one's own blindspots; that the conversational move which says "you're wrong" or "that is not true" is often a conversation-stopper (this last is more a question of tact than fact, however).

Yet it is what we hold true that changes, not truths themselves. The shift from the widely held twelfth-century idea that the earth is flat to the fifteenth-century idea that it is round is not a change in truth but in belief. We now hold that our ancestors had very good reasons for believing what they did about the shape of the earth, indeed little reason for believing anything else. Their beliefs were amply justified, yet wrong. We suspect, furthermore, that if these ancestors were here now and knew what we do, they would agree with us; that between us and them there would be room for dialogue.

So what is truth? We might think, confusedly, that answering this would deliver all the particular truths there are. But as I understand it, the question seeks a clarification of the concept of truth, and this clarification will not tell us which particular propositions are worthy of belief. In short, we cannot give a definition of truth that will allow us to pick out just those propositions that are true. That would be a bit of magic. Nevertheless, we can say clarifying things like the following: truth is a property of sentences, beliefs, propositions, such that if a person's belief that the earth is round is true, the world is round. (Philosophers put it this way: "p" is true if and only if p. For example: the sentence "Miriam is Adrian's sister" is true if and only if Miriam is Adrian's sister.) I will call this idea that truth depends on the way things are, not on how people think they are or wish they were, the homely view of truth. (It is because of this dependency that some philosophers have viewed truth as correspondence. The trouble with this view, however, is that it does not even begin to explain truth; for there is no way of carving out just that part of the world that makes a belief true. This is where coherence comes in. We cannot say that truth just is coherence either, for coherence is only one constraint on rationality. A system of beliefs might be perfectly self-consistent, yet inconsistent with another system. To this, coherentists sometimes respond that any coherent system of beliefs must be appropriately responsive to the way the world is, a response that returns us to the homely idea of truth. For a fuller discussion of truth, correspondence, and coherence, see Cavell, 1993, Chapter One.) Of course, to investigate the truth of any belief or sentence we must first know its meaning, which is constructed by us. Meaning is constructed; so are theories. Furthermore, the meaning of a belief or sentence is constrained by its place in a network of other sentences in the language, or beliefs in the person's mind. But truth is not constructed.

Truth is objective in the sense that the truth of a sentence or belief is independent of us; what is true about a particular matter may be different not only from anybody and everybody's opinion about its truth, but also from its utility: a belief that works for me, even for us, may turn out to be false. (When pushed on this point, pragmatists often retort that "useful" must take in the longest possible run, and everything we will ever know, a retort that collapses "useful" back into "true".)

Here is my claim: subjectivity, in a certain key sense of the word to be defined later, goes hand in hand with intersubjectivity; but also, a concept of intersubjectivity that floats free from the ideas of objectivity and truth is no intersubjectivity at all. This is because of what I see as necessary conditions for the mental. Many psychoanalysts have been saying in different ways that the "space" within which thinking can occur is triangular in character. (I return later to some of these authors.) So I say also; but the space I see is triangulated by one mind, other minds, and the objective world, discoverable by each of them, existing independently of their beliefs and will, a world they share in fact, and which they know they share. The argument I am going to work out is that two minds can know each other as minds only on the same condition. Take away this third point of the triangle, the objective world, and we are left with no minds at all. Give up the idea of an objective reality, "out there" between analyst and patient that we can be more or less objective about, and what we are left with is "the one-person psychology paradigm". Forego the idea that analyst and patient share a common world, despite the differences in their experiences of it, and we make the idea of interpretation unintelligible; for interpretation requires that there be public things, like the words we say, the things we do, the common room that patient and analyst inhabit, to give a common reference from which interpretation can get started, a ground for either agreement or disagreement. I cannot disagree with you about the shape of the earth, for example, unless I know more or less what you mean by "the earth", and believe that we are talking about, more or less, the same thing. If we are not, then we are not disagreeing but talking past each other. The separateness of analyst from patient that is an essential aspect of the psychoanalytic situation is a function of the fact that there is an objective world out there, larger than the two participants, to allow them a perspective beyond their own.

In the first and second sections, I elaborate a certain shift that has taken place in twentieth-century philosophy from what I will call a subjectivist view of meaning and mind to an intersubjectivist view, and I argue for the latter. We find versions of the first in philosophy from Plato, on whom I touch briefly, through Descartes, my central focus, all the way to the contemporary philosopher, John Searle. My discussion of subjectivism attempts to make clear that it is only the Cartesian view of truth from which we need to distance ourselves.

For versions of the intersubjectivist view I single out George Herbert Mead, Vygotsky, Ludwig Wittgenstein, and Donald Davidson. Psychoanalysts familiar with other philosophers who might seem equally well to deserve consideration here, for example, Husserl, Gadamer, Habermas, or Putnam, may wonder why I omit them. I do so for the sake of brevity, and because my view of intersubjectivity is tendentious. The philosophers I discuss are *en route* to the following specific ideas that I think are crucial: (1) the concept of mind can be elucidated only by reference to the normative concepts of truth, objectivity, and reason. This, of course, does not mean that all thought, even of a propositional sort, is rational; much is not. It means, first, that a creature lacking these concepts altogether could not be said to have any thoughts of a propositional sort; it means, second, that so long as there is a mind at all, that mind must be rational to some extent. I will not be arguing the second claim here. (2) When a child can be said to have propositional thought, she has made a qualitative leap from the on-the-way-to-thought child that she was before. The leap describes her, and also our vocabulary for understanding her. (3) To make this leap the child must have been in communication with other (thinking) creatures. This is the sense in which the mind is constituted by an interactive, interpersonal world.

Considerably shorter, the third and fourth sections discuss unconscious fantasy and some problems facing psychoanalysis now. The theme of truth threads through all four sections.

I should make three things clear at the start. First, when I talk about thought, I have in mind desires and emotions as well as beliefs. Second, my concern is specifically with the capacity for thought that is symbolic and propositional in character. Of course, much goes on in the infant prior to the development of this capacity that affects what sort of thinker the child will be. Third, I take for granted that many thoughts, even of a propositional character, are unconscious, and that we all have many thoughts that cannot be captured in words.

The subjectivist view

Plato was struck by the fact that whenever we make a judgement about something—as we do, for example, in believing that this is a table—we use predicates that are general in character. Words and particular ideas mean what they do, Plato thought, by invoking the corresponding general Forms, which transcend material reality and which antedate all human minds. Plato was struck also by the fact that a judgement says something that is in principle true or false. When we know *for certain* which it is, then à propos that judgement, and only then, Plato thought, do we have knowledge; and certainty, like meaning, points to our acquaintance with the transcendent world of Forms. Thus Plato accounts for meaning, truth, and knowledge by appealing to a realm of being that is perfect, timeless, and from which our very corporeality distances us. One important source for the later Christian ideas of original sin, and of atonement (at-one-ment) as requiring an act of divine grace, is here in Plato. (Read "the spatio–temporal body" as what deprives us of godly knowledge.) Nietzsche's famous attack on Truth was fired in part by his belief that the idea of truth is inevitably linked to subservient self-loathing and a denigration of the "merely" human.

Some of Plato's view is discernible in Descartes: for example, the ideas that any knowledge worthy of its name must be certain, and that certainty is underwritten by a transcendent order of reality, which for Descartes was God. But whereas Plato envisaged knowledge as a relation between Mind and the Forms, Descartes substituted a relation between individual mind and its inner ideas or objects.

Descartes asked: given that we are often mistaken in our beliefs, how can we be sure we know anything at all? A part of his answer is that knowledge is guaranteed so long as I claim to know nothing more than the immediate contents of my consciousness. I may be mistaken in thinking that I *believe* the table is red. For to know what I believe I only need turn my mental eye inwards and discern the mental objects that are there: for instance, the idea "the table is red". I will refer to this as the ocular model of self-knowledge. Descartes conceives the mind on the analogy of a theatre, a theatre that only the person whose mind it is can enter. Therefore that person and she alone is in a position to see at first hand what is happening on the stage. But whereas my physical eye sees a table in the material world, normally the same table that you see if you are in the right position, my mental eye sees a thoroughly private, subjective object. These ideas, not the things they supposedly represent, are the only things with which the mind can be acquainted. With Descartes, subjectivity in its modern sense is born, the sense in which our knowledge of our minds is presumably not connected in any essential way with the external world, and in which knowledge of other minds is either impossible or mysterious. (It would be interesting to see how Freud's concept of "das Ich"—"the ego"—implicitly relies on a Cartesian view of the self, even as Freud attempts to change it radically.)

Descartes's picture seems to be in accord with some important phenomena of our mental life, and because it is, the view continues to appeal both to common sense and to some philosophers. It is true, for example, that I can often know what I am thinking about without looking outside myself. So it may seem that the content of an idea is entirely contained within it.

Nevertheless, there are a number of overwhelming problems with the subjectivist paradigm. I will mention a few.

Scepticism: Since it claims that all that we are directly acquainted with is our private, internal representations, the paradigm inevitably leads to scepticism about the very existence of the external world and other minds. (How, indeed, can we even call these ideas "representations"?) Descartes's escape hatch is God, who presumably warrants our knowledge claims if we arrive at them in the right way. Thus, in His goodness, God can close the gap for us between justified belief and true belief. We should note, in passing, that the Cartesian knower is just that "neutral" observer of which many psychoanalysts are now rightly so sceptical, the observer who presumably sees things free of human taint, just as they are, and who can therefore sometimes pronounce with the authority of God.

Meaning and mental content: By the content of a thought I mean what it concerns or is about (I believe this is what Freud (1895) meant by "quality"). Descartes's view of meaning is "internalist" in the sense that he thinks there is no necessary connection, anywhere in the network of a person's thoughts, between mental content and what is outside his mind, between what one means by his words and the external world. The problem here with Descartes is this: if we have no direct acquaintance with the external world but only with our own thoughts, then what entitles us to describe them in a language of material things? What entitles us to say that a particular thought is a world-is-round-sort-of-thought? How can we even speak of our ideas as representations? (To know that one thing represents another, one must have had some experience of both.) Kant might seem to have got around Cartesian scepticism in arguing that there must be a fundamental compatibility between mind and world, and that it is this compatibility that makes knowledge possible. But the distinction Kant draws between the conceptual scheme (imposed by us) and some raw, uninterpreted Given, on which this scheme is imposed, leaves the gap between (subjective) experience and (objective reality) as great as it ever was. To close this gap we need to say, not that we can never know reality perfectly, but that it is reality we apprehend. (For a fuller discussion of representation, "the myth of the Given", and the scheme/content distinction, see Rorty, 1979.)

Historicity: The Cartesian view does not make room for an idea that comes to seem more and more important in the latter part of the nineteenth century; that is, that all knowing is historically situated, necessarily partial in character, the achievement of individuals who are limited by their particular places in space and time. Knowledge is never certain, we now think, and it grows not by transcending partiality altogether but through a dialogue over time.

Language: It is clearly a public phenomenon. The subjectivist begins with the private, internal, and the intrinsically subjective, and will have to account for the publicity of language by somehow matching public words to private states or objects. But since in his view these states are thoroughly internal, it is hard to see how any such matching can take place.

To be sure, there are philosophers who think these problems can be solved in very different ways from the ones I suggest. I cannot argue with them here. My aim rather is to sketch an approach to mind and meaning that to many of us looks very promising, an approach that starts with public phenomena, like people doing things with each other, and works its way "inward" to mind.

Before leaving subjectivism, I should point out that Freud unquestioningly accepted the Cartesian ocular model of self-knowledge (somewhat modified by Kant), together with its scepticism about our knowledge of the external world. Freud writes: "Consciousness makes each of us aware only of his own states of mind" (1915e, p. 169). And also,

> behind the attributes of the object under examination which are presented directly to perception, we have to discover something else which is more independent of the particular receptive capacity of our sense organs and which approximates more closely to what may be supposed to be the real state of affairs. We have no hope of being able to reach the latter itself. [1940a (1938)]

And again:

[psychical reality] is as much unknown to us as the reality of the external world, and it is as incompletely presented by the data of unconsciousness as is the external world by the communication of our sense organs. [1900a, p. 613]

The intersubjectivist view and the normativity of the mental

One of the first thinkers to put forward an intersubjectivist position was G. H. Mead. Influenced by Darwin, Mead attempted to give a naturalistic account of specifically human thought by tracing it to lower, simpler orders of communication (Mead, 1934). At the same time, he insisted that our symbolizing activity is categorically different from any form of communication from which it evolves. The (impossible) problem he set himself was, in effect, to reduce the irreducible (more about reducibility later).

Mead distinguishes three levels of meaning. The first he calls a conversation of gestures, seen among the higher vertebrates. The second is the signal-language level at which a single word like "fire", for example, acts as a stimulus to behaviour. The third level is fully articulated propositional thought in which symbols, which are not context-dependent, replace signals that are.

In a conversation of gestures, the evolutionary starting point, two animals respond to each other reciprocally, the behaviour of each acting as a stimulus to the other. In a dog-fight, for example, the behaviour of Fido prompts a second dog to act in a way that in turn modifies Fido's behaviour, and so on. The two dogs are inter-acting in a way that resembles human conversation, but we do not think their "gestures" are accompanied by ideas in their heads; it is we, the observers, who ascribe meanings to animal behaviour on the basis of what function it has within a group: searching for food, defending against predators, finding a mate, and so on.

An essential difference between a mere gesture and gesture at the symbolic level, Mead holds, is that the latter is accompanied by an idea, an idea that is virtually the same for both creatures. (The patient says, "I am feeling depressed", and if the analyst catches his meaning, she thinks something like "He is feeling depressed".) To explain how symbolic communication evolves from the conversa-tion of gestures, Mead posits an identificatory act that he calls "taking the attitude of the other". The basic idea is that a gesture of the first creature, A, takes on a meaning for the second creature, B, who responds to A's gesture; in so doing, B interprets A's gesture in a certain way. A did not intend his gesture to have such a meaning; he did not intend anything at all. Yet if A can now take B's attitude towards his own gesture, he becomes his own interpreter; his gesture acquires for him a meaning like that it has for B. I have cast the process Mead envisions as if it took place in the life of a single individual, but Mead thinks of it as spanning species and generations. At the end of this process, he thinks, a creature with symbolic thought has evolved.

With the ideas of "internalizing" and "taking the attitude of the other", Mead hoped to have located a particular bit of behaviour that would explain the rise of symbolic thought, while preserving his insight that it is irreducible to anything less complex. But it is a pseudo-explanation; for either A's taking the attitude of the other is just the very thing to be explained, an act of interpretation that presumes symbolic thought, or else there is nothing yet to distinguish what A does from mimicry or imitation, and we have not left the conversation of gesture. Nevertheless, in launching an investigation of meaning from two creatures interacting in a shared world, Mead's argument moves in the right direction. By implication, Descartes's investigation was wrong-headed both because it made the solitary individual its starting point, and because it took reflection rather than purposive, worldly action as the paradigmatic expression of human thought.

During roughly the same period of time, the Russian psychologist Vygotsky was developing an idea similar to Mead's. Vygotsky also held that the individual mind emerges from a more rudimentary and collective form of life, and that the crucial turn is a kind of internalization of the other. Critical of Piaget, who held, following Freud, that first there are deeply personal, subjective, autistic mental states, which under the pressure of socialization finally yield to "social thought", Vygotsky traced a developmental scheme that proceeds from social communication, to egocentric thought, and finally to full-fledged mental states (Vygotsky, 1962). Vygotsky writes: "the process of internalisation is not the *transferral* of an external activity to a pre-existing internal plane of consciousness; it is the process in which this internal plane is formed" (quoted in

Wertsch, 1985, p. 64). For example: the child reaches unsuccessfully for an object, and the mother comes to get the object for the child. Over time what was at first a gesture that had no significance for the child but only for the mother, becomes, through that interaction, a gesture with which the child *means* to point.[1] By this route, eventually the child as well as the mother can point to the apple with the idea in mind, "Here is an apple". Daniel Stern's use of the idea of feedback loops in parent–infant interactions might suggest a similar process (Stern, 1995).

Like Mead and Vygotsky, the later Wittgenstein thought the traditional subjectivist picture was fundamentally wrong-headed in isolating thought from action, private thought from public speech, mind from body, and one mind from other minds. The Platonic idea that individual words or concepts have meaning all by themselves begins its investigation of meaning in the wrong place, for words come to have meaning only through the activities of actual speakers who are doing things with words in the course of carrying out communal enterprises (Wittgenstein, 1953). Attention to the ways language is actually used in daily life will free us from the temptation to hypostatize language and meanings, as Plato did in positing a heaven of Forms. There are not *meanings*, but people meaning things by what they say and do.

To see how a view about meaning might take us to the intersubjectivist claim that the mind is constituted out of its interactions with other creatures, recall Descartes' ocular view of the mind, that each of us knows what she thinks (what she means)—when she does—by looking inwards. The presupposition here is that the meaning of an idea is written on its face. Ideas have the content they do through representing something else. But, Wittgenstein points out, the concept of representation does not help in explaining how words and ideas acquire meaning; what a sign represents is not something the sign itself can tell us. Even a portrait of Marilyn Monroe that is very faithful to her can be taken to be her portrait only by someone who knows something about Monroe. And, of course, many representations are not isomorphic with the things they represent. For a representation of an apple, say, *to be* a representation of an apple, the person for whom it represents an apple must intend it to do so, must know its meaning already. So the idea of representation leaves unexplained the very thing it was meant to elucidate: how signs, words, ideas, thoughts, come to have the meaning they do.

To take another tack, supposedly our inner life is what we most intimately and, sometimes, more surely know. This is the datum from which Cartesianism begins. But how does a child ever learn the concept of pride, for example? How does it begin to learn that it feels proud, and to be able to say to itself, "I feel proud"? There must be intrinsic connections between behaviour and concepts like belief, desire, anger, sadness, pride, if a child is able to acquire such concepts. My pride is known to me in a peculiar way, but it also has an objective aspect, transforming me as an object for others. If this were not so, no one could ever learn the language of mind. The more interesting argument—I think it can be made but will not attempt it here—is that the child learns not merely to name pride but to feel it through social interactions. (Anxiety and rage are among the emotions that in their most primitive form are not constructed through interpersonal interactions.)

Wittgenstein is not denying that my experience of pride, or sadness, or pain, is peculiar to me, nor that we can sometimes keep our pains and thoughts to ourselves, two ideas that the concept of subjectivity captures. He is insisting that unless the child were in communion with other creatures who had pains, who sometimes expressed them in their behaviour, and who recognized that the child has experiences similar to the adult's, the child could not learn the concept of pain. She could not even think the thought, "I am in pain", or "Mama is in pain". We use the word "subjectivity" in many ways; in some, it is attributable to infants and creatures other than ourselves. But in the non-Cartesian sense of "subjectivity" that I am singling out, subjectivity exists only where there is the having of thoughts, some of which one knows as *thoughts*, and as his *own* thoughts. In this sense, about which I will say more shortly, subjectivity is not a condition into which we are born but one we slowly enter through our interactions with the world and with other persons in this world.

When one already has a mind of one's own, it remains the case that others can sometimes know us in a way we cannot know ourselves; this is one implication of the concept of unconscious mental processes, and one reason why other persons cay play an important role in the acquisition of self-knowledge. If I am a patient in analysis, the only truths about me that will do me any good are truths I myself possess. But sometimes a first step in my knowing, for example, that I am sad, and being able to link up a feeling with the thoughts that make it comprehensible to me, may be somebody else's pointing out to me that I seem to be sad. Modell writes of the ways in which "the growing child requires the confirmation of the *other* to claim possession of her affect", and remarks that the analyst does something analogous for his patient (1990, p. 72).

Wittgenstein does not investigate in detail the personal inter-actions leading to subjectivity; he implies that such an investigation would include the ways in which other people's responses to the child shape his emerging sense of himself, and so the understand-ing that he brings to his eventual first-person thinking. These are just the sorts of interactions that, because of its essentially inter-personal character, the psychoanalytic dialogue can bring to light. For example, Winnicott tells the story of a male patient who knows himself to be male, but who talks as if what he were feeling were penis envy. Winnicott says to him, "I am listening to a girl. I know perfectly well that you are a man but I am listening to a girl, and talking to a girl. I am telling this girl, 'You are talking about penis envy'. After a pause, the patient responds, "If I were to tell some-one about this girl I would be called mad". Winnicott claims the madness as his—that is, as that of the mother who had wanted this boy to be a girl—and goes on to say, "This madness which was mine enabled him to see himself as a girl *from my position*" (Winnicott, 1971, pp. 73–74).

I have said that learning a mental vocabulary presumes inter-action with other people. Yet, so far, Wittgenstein's argument does not obviously unsettle our (Cartesian) assumption that language is merely a (public) tool with which we attempt to communicate thoughts, many of which are intrinsically private. Wittgenstein does have a more general argument, which unfortunately is extremely elusive, and much debated. As I see it, the argument begins with the assumption that only behaviour that is guided or informed by concepts can be said to be "minded". It goes on to say that one grasps a concept only if one knows how to follow a rule that tells us how to apply the concept, and that the measure of knowing how to follow a rule is being able to go on applying it as other creatures do. As Wittgenstein puts it, "It is not possible to obey a rule 'privately'; otherwise thinking one was obeying a rule would be the same thing as obeying it" (1953, par. 202). If the argument worked, it would indeed show that no creature can have concepts, or thoughts of a conceptual nature, in the absence of communication with other creatures. It would show that a child whose physical needs were taken care of but who was raised without communication with others could not know its own mind because it would not have a mind to know.

But why should we invest the ability to follow a rule with this significance? What does Wittgenstein mean by "following a rule" Clearly something other than the mere disposition to do as others do; bees and lemmings and indeed all other creatures are so disposed, yet we can describe their behaviour without ascribing to them concepts. Nor does discriminatory behaviour, by itself, indicate the presence of concepts, for, in their absence, sunflowers can turn towards the sun, thermostats register degrees of heat, bulls be enraged by the colour red.

The relationship between being a creature that can follow rules and being a creature whose behaviour is guided by concepts becomes clearer if we say this: having concepts (in the sense Wittgenstein is trying to capture) presumes the creature's understanding that some things are *correctly* included under the concept and some things are not, that some applications of it are right, and some wrong, for this would begin to explain the link Wittgenstein sees between having concepts and the ability to follow a rule. An infant might wave its hands in a particular way only when it is handed a rattle, but many of us would not want to say that therefore the infant has the concept of a rattle. So I read Wittgenstein as making the following suggestion: let us speak of the child's having the concept of a rattle not only when it responds selectively to rattles, but when it can think something like "this is a rattle" and also "that is *not* a rattle". Wittgenstein is suggesting that concepts—and the sort of thinking that uses concepts, *propositional* thinking—come along only with the normative concepts of error, correct and incorrect, right and wrong. Like "subjectivity", "concept" too can be defined in many ways. But the concepts Wittgenstein has in mind presumably emerge only in specifically human contexts, through engagement in those worldly forms of life of which he so evocatively speaks.

Both the claims that thinking has an essentially normative character, and that only a social situation can provide a field in which
this normativity arises, are more clearly argued in Davidson. It is in
his light that I have presented Wittgenstein. Before turning to him,
we should ask: why is propositional thought so important? Because
only thought of a propositional sort has implications, makes asser-
tions, sometimes contradicts itself, makes promises and reneges on
promises, commits the thinker to certain conclusions (whether he
accepts them or not), is open to doubt, challenge, question, reflection. Only propositional thought makes a place for dialogue that is
both personal and intrapersonal: I can wonder what I mean by
what I said, and I can also ask you what you mean by what you
said. It is only thinking of this sort that can be either rational or irra-
tional (as distinct from a-rational); self-deceptive, or foreclosing
reflection, or repressing what one knows, or dissociating some
thoughts from others. What is involved in having belief that is
propositional in character, Davidson asks? The answer goes something like this: to believe that "p" just is to hold that "p" is true.
Of course, you can know that it might be false, can be doubtful
of its truth, and so on; the point is that the concepts of belief and
truth, evidence and reason, are necessarily linked. So, if you have
a belief or a propositional sort (the beliefs we may attribute to other
animals than ourselves are presumably not propositional in character), you must have a grasp of the distinction between how you
think things are and how they (truly) are, between right and
wrong, correct and incorrect, true and false, since belief is, by
definition, a state of mind about the world; it is the sort of thing
that, by definition, can be true or false (even though one may never
know in a particular case which it is), and for which one adduces
evidence and reasons. (Whatever conditions provide for the possibility of belief, provide also, in my view, for the possibility of
fantasy, if by fantasy we mean a mental state ascribable only to
a creature that has some beliefs.) The goal, then, is to say what we
can about how a child might get hold of the distinctions between
the false and the true, between how things seem and how they
objectively are.

There must be a kind of triangulating process, as Davidson calls
it (1989, 1992), in which child and adult communicate—at first,
not in words on the child's part, of course—about an object in the

physical world they share. To see how triangulation works, Davidson sketches a primitive learning situation. The mother hands the child an apple, saying "apple" as she does. Mother and child are together interested in the apple, and interested also in each other's response to it. The child babbles, and at some point, in this or a similar transaction, the child hits on a sound close enough to "apple" so that the mother rewards the child—with a laugh, intensified interest, more play, or any of the other kinds of responses that infant observers have described. In time we can give content to the mother's saying that the child is responding specifically to applies. The mother has in mind the apple when she says "apple", and apple is what she means by the word.

The question, however, was the point at which we can say that "apple" is what the child himself means, and, so far, there is nothing to distinguish the mother's response to the child from an observer's response to a trained dog. so our story about the child needs a more complex form of triangulation than the one we have yet described. What it needs is a very particular sort of interaction between child and mother, in which they can observe an object in common, and observe also each other's responses to that common object. The child must be responding to a specific object, and he must know that the mother is responding to that same object. Over time, the child can then correlate the mother's responses to the object with his own. (Winnicott's writings about the transitional object are on to a similar idea. The concept of reality is constructed for any child, Winnicott suggests, through her triangular interactions with some loved external object and a loved other person who is responding both to her and to that same object. Such an object can then become symbolic, say of the breast. Winnicott writes, "When symbolism is employed, the infant is already clearly distinguishing between fantasy and fact, between inner objects and external objects, between primary creativity and perception" [Winnicott, 1971, p. 6]. Yet, while Winnicott thinks that before this time there are inner objects, I want to say that only when there are, for the child, objects that are truly public can there also be "objects" that are truly inner in a subjective, inner world.)

So the object must be something public, discernible by both mother and child, to which, furthermore, they can give a name that will allow them both to refer to it even in its absence. They must be responding to the same object in the world; they must be responding to it in similar ways; and they must both observe that they are. In such a situation it will sometimes be the case that mother and child respond to the same thing—something they can both see to be the same thing—differently. The questions can then arise: who is right, she or I? What is the object really like? What does she see that I do not? Or, what do I see that she does not? It is this sort of situation that makes room for the normative concepts of error, right and wrong, true and false, "my view of things" versus "hers", "my view" versus "the way things (objectively) are". (It *makes room* for these concepts; it does not fully explain them, a caveat I return to in a moment. And at some point this child may learn that there is no such thing as a view of the object from *nowhere*.) Such an interaction not only allows the mother, or any interpreter, Sarah, to say of John, "he is seeing an x"; it allows John to say of himself, as it were, "I am seeing an x" (or "I want an x", or "I am thinking about an x"). The belief that there is an apple on the table draws a line from oneself to the world. But what fixes the terms joined by the line? If we say, "I and the thing itself", there is nothing to give me the idea of it as an *object* external to me that can be seen from different perspectives.

This picture of what is needed for concept formation begins with the claim, which many philosophers in this century have made, that mental content is partly constituted by the events in the world that are its cause. (This is not something that Descartes maintained. Whatever the causal relations between external and internal world, they are, in his view, not in any way intrinsic to the content of that internal world.) But events in the world have causal impact on sunflowers and lemmings, without this impact taking the form of concepts. So the question is, what is needed to begin to bridge the gap between mere causal relation and an object or event in the world that the child can conceive as such? What is needed to allow the cause—say the rattle, or the apple—to enter into what Wilfred Sellars called "the space of reasons"? What allows the stimulus— light from an apple on the table reaching my eye—to become a belief, a perception of the form "I see *that* there is an apple on the table"? What is needed to baptise this cause with a name, and a name, furthermore, that has meaning for the two players—where meaning, as we have seen, is itself a normative notion? This is the question to which the triangulation picture suggests a partial answer. As Richard Rorty recently wrote,

> The key to understanding the relation between minds and bodies is not an understanding of the irreducibility of the intentional to the physical but the understanding of the inescapability of a normative vocabulary. For the inability by an organism to use such a vocabulary entails that that organism is not using language at all. ["Davidson between Wittgenstein and Tarski", unpublished]

My own triangulation argument differs from Davidson's in claiming that the child needs not just one but two other persons, one of whom, at least in theory, might be only the child's idea of a third. To have the distinctions between true and false, thought and world, the child must move from interacting with his mother to grasping the idea that both his perspective on the world and hers are *perspectives*; that there is a possible third point of view, more inclusive than theirs, from which both his mother's and his own can be seen and from which the interaction between them can be understood. One prerequisite for this is the experience of sometimes being responded to in an appropriate way, as Wittgenstein also suggested. Another prerequisite is observing disagreement between other persons.

The grasp of this third possible point of view is also part of what allows for such perplexing adult attitudes as self-forgiveness. Someone can experience forgiveness if she is forgiven by the person she feels she has wronged. But if he does not forgive her, or if he is dead, then forgiveness can come only from oneself, which seems to present the insurmountable problem of getting outside one's own skin. A solution is in sight when one becomes able, imaginatively, to occupy a position beyond herself from which her actions do not appear as isolated "bad" fragments, but as interactions with another person, each with complex wishes and needs. One needs to see not only oneself as a whole, but also the relationship between oneself and the other. In having such a third-person perspective, the analyst can help her patient begin to discover one like it.

Now I can say more about that sense of subjectivity that I am urging comes only with intersubjectivity. A creature has subjectivity in this sense when it knows some of its beliefs as *beliefs*, and as its *own* beliefs. This means, as Wittgenstein and others have argued, that it is able to make attributions of mental states to others (see Strawson, 1963, Part III; Evans, 1982, Chapter Six); it understands that the mental states of another are available to him in a way they are not to one's self, as one's own thoughts are accessible to one's self in a way they are not to others. Such a child, as Fonagy puts it (following Premack and Woodruff), has "a theory of mind" (Fonagy, 1989), and only such a creature can distinguish, some of the time, between playing and reality, fantasy and fact. (I would say, further-more, that only when that distinction is in place does the concept of fantasy have any clear meaning, but I am not arguing that here.)

Of course, these knowings that characterize the very having of a mind, a mind that is one's own, are fragile, vulnerable, easily disturbed. We do not always recognize a fantasy for what it is (that we do not is one of the defining characteristics of fantasy in its specifically psychoanalytic sense); particularly if we are children, we confusedly fantasize that our own minds are transparent to others, and we confuse wishing something were so with making it so. But these are vicissitudes of mind, not the natural condition of a particular sort of (disturbed) mind. As Fonagy writes,

> Although borderline patients' capacity to differentiate self and other is legitimately described as impaired and "boundaries" between the two can be said to be blurred, those descriptions do not do justice to the complexity of the mechanisms involved. Even frank psychotics know that the person they are talking to is a separate person. [1989, p. 109]

But what about—one will rightly ask—the subjectivity of children for whom all of this is not yet in place? Can we not ask what the world is like for them? And may not the answer bear on the sort of thinking, reflective, self-aware persons they will become? Of course, Fonagy, Stern, Emde, and others who have observed infants have asked these questions and begun to suggest some interesting answers. From these writers we have learned that early infant–parent exchanges have a great deal to do, for example, with whether the child begins to feel that he can, or cannot, make himself understood; that he has or does not have something valuable to say or to give (a child who is not noticed, not listened to, may come to

believe, by way of defending his parent, and himself from catas-
trophic anger towards her, that he is not worthy of being understood); that he is more or less at home in the world, or, dangerously
omnipotent, at its edge. But I would describe all this as a matter of
habits of attention or avoidance, of response and the evoking of
response in others, of perception and feeling, that have a lot to do
both with how the child will come to sense himself and the world,
and with how reflective and thoughtful a person he will become,
but that are set up prior to thought *per se*.

There are obvious similarities between the concept of triangulation I am urging and those of a number of psychoanalytic writers.
Thus, Ronald Britton (following Bion) writes that the child's
acknowledgement of the parents' relationship with each other
creates "a triangular space" in which thinking can occur (Britton,
1989). Green writes that Winnicott's "transitional object" describes
not so much "an object as a space lending itself to the creation of
objects" (Green, 1993, p. 285). Ogden develops a concept of "the
analytic third", according to which the analyst gives voice to the
experience of the analysand as experienced by the analyst (Ogden,
1994, Chapter Five), thus providing, as I think of it, a third perspective from which the analysand can see himself. My picture of triangulation differs from Britton's and Green's in insisting not only on
the presence of persons besides the child, but also on a real external world, common to them both. Furthermore, language has a
central place in triangulation as I conceive it, for it is through
language and language-learning that triangulation takes place.
Child, mother, and world interact in such a way that concepts,
belief, and propositional thought come into being for the first time.
Some "knowledge" of syntax may be innate, as Chomsky and
others have argued. But no one has successfully shown that mental
content is innate. Language is not a robe that the child casts over
his thought, but the medium through which he engages with others
and the world in the way that begins to constitute mental life.

It is important to point out that the triangulation argument gives
only a necessary condition for thought and not its necessary and
sufficient conditions, which is to say that a creature might inhabit
the situation that triangulation describes and yet not develop
thought. This is one of the reasons for my saying that thought is
irreducible to any of the prior conditions that we can specify for it,

without covertly including thought itself among them. The search for something more, for necessary *and* sufficient conditions, is very tempting: since mind obviously cannot come into being unless all the physical properties and worldly conditions necessary to sustain it are present, one might hope to identify mind with these conditions or some subset of them. The present interest in consciousness seems to be motivated by such a hope: surely there must be, some philosophers, psychoanalysts, and neurologists think, some particular set of neural connections that will explain consciousness so thoroughly that we can say, this *is* consciousness. But mind, subjectivity, thought, consciousness, truth, and so on, all confront us with what Polanyi calls "emergent properties" (Polanyi, 1958), properties that in a developmental process arise spontaneously from elements at the preceding levels and are not specifiable or predictable in terms of them.

When we can attribute propositional thoughts to a child, I have argued, we must also be attributing to it the concepts of "the objectively real", "true" and "false", "my perspective" and "your perspective", all of which concepts arise only within the language of mind; and for none of these concepts can we supply necessary and sufficient conditions in some other language. In this sense, all these concepts arise together; in particular it is not the case that the child first grasps the concept of himself and then the concept of an other person. (Daniel Stern's claim [1984] that there is from the beginning a sense of self is ambiguous: a "sense" of self is not necessarily the recognition of oneself as an "I", with all that is involved in knowing the use of the first-person pronoun. In any case it is a claim that Stern acknowledges he cannot substantiate.) Wittgenstein wrote (1972, para 141), "When we first begin to *believe* anything, what we believe is not a single proposition, it is a whole system of propositions. (Light dawns gradually over the whole.)" By the time the *whole* over which the dawn comes is fully lit, the child has made a quantum leap.

Mead descried a categorical difference between a conversation of gestures and one that can be adequately described only in the language of mind. He hoped to bridge the gap with an act of identification or internalization. But as I pointed out earlier, he begged the question by answering it with the very thing to be explained. This must be the fate of all attempts to specify an emergent property in terms of things at a lower level. For this reason, if Bion's project (1962) is to trace a continuous line from primitive "thoughts" to thinking, it fails: either we have abstracted these thoughts from something that is already a thinking process, or they are so distant from it that thinking itself cannot provide a bridge. It is true that all of us are unable to think about some of our thoughts; but they occur in a mental setting in which we can think about some. We cannot extrapolate backwards from fantasies or thoughts, unrecognized as such, to a time of thoughts before there was any thinking.

Nevertheless, though it does not fully explain propositional thought, the triangulation argument illuminates it in the following ways: it works against the subjectivist view of the mind in telling us that the child comes to have thoughts *about* the world or to make judgements about it only as he comes to be an interpreter of others; and it indicates that such acts of interpretation require a shared world and the concept of objectivity. Mead's deep insight was that there is an intrinsic connection between being interpreted by another and being an interpreter oneself, between interpretation and symbolic thought. Neither interpreting others nor thinking for oneself could exist in isolation. Since reason is a parameter of any conversation between creatures who think, I will call it a dialogue to distinguish it from a conversation of gestures. Unlike the latter, dialogue creates and presumes a shared conceptual space in which something of common interest can be talked about together, and only a dialogue is genuinely intersubjective in the sense that each participant knows himself as an "I", a subject who can think of himself as a self, and knows the other as a subject, an "I" for himself.

Towards the beginning of this paper I said that the concept of reality loses its sense in the absence of a distinction between how things seem to me or to us, and how things are, and I promised to say why we need such a concept for our human lives. The answer is that a creature who could not grasp this distinction, in principle (though not always in a particular case), would necessarily lack the idea that another's experience of the world is different from one's own, so lack both the idea of subjectivity and that capacity for empathy that takes for granted the uniqueness of every person's perspective. Such a creature could not recognize its beliefs as *beliefs*, rather than simply the way the world is. So it would lack also the concepts of evidence and reasons, the capacities for reflection and for dialogue.

Here is how things look on the intersubjectivist account I am presenting. The concepts of right and wrong, true and false, do not enter our minds from some Platonic or Judeo-Christian heaven, but emerge from within an interpersonal, worldly, situation. This does not mean that truth is just a convention, or what the majority holds true; it is perfectly possible for the majority to be mistaken on any particular issue. On just this possibility the distinction between things as they appear to me, *or to us,* insists. A convention is a practice we can change, or can imagine changing; but there is no imaginable alternative to the concept of truth that will do the job we human creatures need to do—argue things out, assess evidence, look for reasons, disagree with each other, find a consensus, questions our own convictions, and so on. Which beliefs we hold true, of course, differ from person to person; so also our ways of discovering the truth, and what we count as evidence. But the concept of truth does not. Both the proverbial Trobrian Islander and speaker of Standard English implicitly understand that a claim about *what is* calls for evidence and reasons (they may differ about whether a particular reason is bad or good, or whether a particular test captures evidence that is relevant to the issue at hand). In short, both believers share roughly the same methodology. Then, having come into a condition of dialogue with the other, the anthropologist might even discuss with his informant whether his beliefs are true, just as the psychoanalyst may also with her patient. This is not necessarily a dead-end question, since an ongoing conversation in which you and I come to understand better *what* each of us believes may in fact lead to a change of mind. It is in just this way that changes in what we *hold* to be true come about.

The seventeenth-century ideal of scientific objectivity posited an observer who does not affect or intrude upon the object of his investigation. We have abandoned that ideal. But another, to which I think all analysts do hold fast, asks us to try to distinguish between fantasy and reality and to take the viewpoints of others into account. With Aron, we might now view analytic neutrality as "the analyst's openness to new perspectives, a commitment to take other perspectives seriously, and a refusal to view any interpretation as complete, or any meaning as exhaustive" (Aron, 1996, p. 28).

Our developmental picture looks something like this: from the very beginning, infants make sounds and gestures that their caretakers take as signs of the infant's wants and needs. But the infant only gradually becomes able himself to mean something by what he says and does. The implication is not that before the infant has propositional thoughts and intentional states, nothing at all is going on in its head. Infants have feelings, emotions, sensations, purposes, instincts; they communicate, perceive, and learn. Once again, infant research is useful here in showing how patterns of interaction between infant and caretaker can very early establish habits of response that later might be expressed as core beliefs such as "I had better not let on that I know what I know", or "I deserve every bad thing that happens to me", or "I am [or am not] able to cope with new tasks", or "the world is a fearful [or an exciting] place".

The practices of interpreting another, asking him and oneself for evidence and reasons, pointing out that this remark or this judgement is not consistent with others, mark the very space of reasons the child enters, and must enter, in learning how to think. Of course, the interpersonal relations that initiate the child into it are not coolly rational but fraught with other lessons about loving and losing, abandoning and being lost, wanting and not having, and these lessons often fetter one's thinking ability. Psychoanalysis very well describes our initiations into thought, not by picturing a space alternative to that of reasons, but more of what the space of reasons is like.

Fantasy and the foreclosure of thinking

I have said that subjectivity in a certain specific sense—my having thoughts that I sometimes know as thoughts and as mine—comes along with some understanding of the world as public and shared, which we interpret in some shared ways. I now want to distinguish this general sense of subjectivity from another. The first words the child learns are public; the language she grows up speaking is also sufficiently public for her often to make herself understood. But because no two people are alike, any concept quickly acquires resonances that are unique to the child; so at the same time as she learns to mean something by her words and communicate that meaning to others, the child is acquiring an idiolect, a way of thinking, that is hers alone. Some of this is unconscious.

The trouble with that part of the inner world which is neurotic is that dialogue, intersubjective testing, even reflection by the agent herself, are foreclosed. This is the status with neurotic fantasies; they are fixed, frozen in time, apparently (so they seem to the person herself) among the *givens* of the world, like the objects that we find there. We do not recognize them as our thoughts about the objects that we find. (Whether or not one accepts Melanie Klein's account of the infant's inner world, it aptly depicts the way in which unconscious fantasies can strike the person herself as things embedded in the mind, or as the lining of the mind, rather than as the mind's own thoughts.) As distinct from fantasizing, thinking allows for self-reflection and for appraising one's own thoughts as true or false, realistic or unrealistic, and so on. We think with thoughts, about things, and we cannot think about these things unless we recognize our thoughts about them as thoughts. Someone gripped by a fantasy has for the moment put aside the possibility that what he thinks might be false, or a case of wishful thinking, or just a partial view of things. He has put aside questions of evidence and reasons. One of the therapist's tasks is to engage him in such a way that what was a fantasy can become instead a belief, and as such, subject to reflection and doubt; to free important other persons in his world from their frozen status in fantasy so that, in Loewald's memorable image, ghosts (haunting the patient's mind) can become ancestors (in the real and public world).

The goal may be accomplished partly through the way in which, in transference, the patient attempts to plug the analyst into the world as he, the patient, has unknowingly constructed it. The analyst feels, through countertransference, something of what the patient wants from her; at the same time she is learning his idiolect through listening to his dreams, images, and associations. So the analyst both learns to speak in a way the patient can understand, and refuses to play the role that she is asked to play in his fantasy world. The analytic process is sometimes described as giving the patient more choice. Before, he did not know what he was doing; now that he does, he can for the first time choose whether to go on doing it. But as Jonathan Lear (1993) points out, this misdescribes the process: when one sees that what one had taken as just the way things are is instead one's own way of looking at the world, "just the way things are" can no longer survive as *simply that*. This world collapses. It is replaced by a space for thinking about the way things are.

The claim that all experiences are equally subjective—thought trivially true—has the effect of flattening, *for the analyst*, the distinctions she needs between the publicly available and the privately constructed. The claim can also lead to confusions about the nature of empathy, which I understand as the ability, temporarily, to experience the world more as less as another does, not by forgetting the other's particular vantage point but precisely by having a good sense of it, at the same time as one holds on to one's own perceptions and one's own methodology for testing them, a *methodology that in the broadest sense is the same as the patient's*. The patient's fantasies are *fantasies* because he does not, or refuses to, query them in the way we query, at least when the occasion arises, our fully conscious belief and desires. If the analyst treats all the patient's convictions as having equal validity among themselves, and with her own, she in effect colludes with him in keeping his fantasies untested (Grossman, 1996); she is in no position to point out that some of his convictions conflict with his own beliefs, and also with his own understanding of what gives a belief validity, which is not its actual truth (this is always open to question), but his having submitted it to dialogue with another or himself. These are ways in which analyst and patient share a common methodology.

There are, of course, other forms of irrationality than unconscious fantasy, and all of them make sense only linked to the concepts of truth and falsity. Self-deception, for example, sometimes consists in allowing oneself to hold on to a belief in one part of one's mind, so to speak, that in another one thinks is false. Resistance sometimes consists in holding at bay a perception one fears may be true.

Where we are now

Why would anybody deny the homely view of truth, as the pragmatists Peirce, James, Dewey, and, recently, Rorty, have seemed to do? And why would many psychoanalysts, particularly those who count themselves as "relationalists" or as "intersubjectivists", have jumped on the pragmatist bandwagon? My remarks on the history of philosophy were an attempt to answer the first question by saying that the pragmatists were reacting to a view of meaning that ignores its roots in human interests, and holds that reason, divinely guided, can find certainty. We can call this truth with a capital T. Rorty, in particular, thinks we have to turn our backs on the philosophical tradition that thought of truth as correspondence with something outside the mind, something to which we do not have direct access. Showing how a theory of mind can banish truth as correspondence, and how that very theory must hold on to the concept of truth as defining the concepts of belief and mind, is something that cannot be done here. I hope to have given some idea of the lines the argument would take. (For a longer answer, see Davidson, 1984.)

The second question has to be set in the context of the very difficult problems now facing psychoanalysis. Viewing therapeutic change as to some extent brought about by new, collaborative constructions in the present rather than by accurate reconstructions of the past, seeing insight as a creating as much as a finding, psychoanalysts are confronted with some philosophical puzzles about what the self and self-discovery are. And, in the course of questioning many of the hypotheses Freud thought definitive of his "science", among them, drive theory and the centrality of the oedipal complex, psychoanalysts have generated a plurality of theories, some of which are clearly incompatible with each other. In thinking about the important question, "what is it this particular patient is warding off?", for example, the analyst has to make some choices, as she does also in sorting through the various competing theories, both about the mind and about how it can change through therapy.

In his discontent with the imperfections of human knowledge, Descartes turned away from the external world. He replaced external objects and real other minds with internal objects which we can know, he thought, for sure. The "two-person" psychology of the intersubjectivists is at war with old-fashioned (Cartesian) authoritarianism. It insists that what matters to us is not some timeless other world but the human here-and-now. Yet, interestingly, to say that "reality" refers only to something "subjective" is just the "about-face" that Descartes made. And it suggests, with Descartes, that if we play our cards right, we need no longer be troubled that another person, or the future, may prove us wrong.

If we cannot get rid of truth, then we cannot abandon the sorts of questions that a concern with truth asks, like: what evidence is there to think that a particular theory is true? Is it compatible with something else we hold true? Are you and I perhaps both deluded, or thinking wishfully? As Glen Gabbard has recently pointed out (1997), the question of analytic "objectivity" is not without its clinical implications. My guess is that in their practice, most psychoanalysts honour the distinctions between justified belief and true belief, also between what works and what is the case. These distinctions call, however, for a different account of truth than the one some psychoanalysts have championed, often in the name of openness to other points of view. There is talk now of the way in which analyst and patient "co-construct reality". Each of us constructs *a picture* of reality. Reality is what keeps pulling us back to the drawing board.

Note

1. Ferenczi was on to a similar idea in "Stages in the development of the sense of reality" (1956). In the third, he says, the infant learns that some of its wants will be answered if it makes the right signals. Putting Ferenczi's point in another way, what is initially a cry without meaning to the crier becomes meaningful to him in part through the behaviour it produces in another.

References

Aron, L. (1996). *A Meeting of Minds, Mutuality in Psychoanalysis.* Hillsdale, NJ: Analytic Press.

Bion, W. R. (1962). The psycho-analytic study of thinking. *International Journal of Psychoanalysis, 43*: 306–310.

Britton, R. (1989). The missing link: parental sexuality in the Oedipus complex. In: J. Steiner (Ed.), *The Oedipus Complex Today* (pp. 83–101). London: Karnac.

Cavell, M. (1993). *The Psychoanalytic Mind. From Freud to Philosophy.* Cambridge, MA: Harvard University Press.

Davidson, D. (1984). *Inquiries into Truth and Interpretation.* Oxford: Clarendon.

Davidson, D. (1989). The conditions of thought. In: J. Brandl & W. L. Gombocz (Eds.), *The Mind of Donald Davidson.* Amsterdam: Rodopi.

Davidson, D. (1992). The second person. *Midwest Studies in Philosophy, XVII*: 255–267.

Evans, G. (1982). *The Varieties of Reference.* Oxford: Oxford University Press.

Ferenczi, S. (1956). Stages in the development of the sense of reality. In: C. Newton (Trans.), *Sex in Psychoanalysis* (pp. 213–239). New York: Dover.

Fogel, G. I., Tyson, P., Greenberg, J., McLaughlin, J. T., & Peyser, E. R. (1996). A classic revisited: Loewald on the therapeutic action of psychoanalysis. *Journal of the American Psychoanalytic Association, 44*: 863–924.

Fonagy, P. (1989). On tolerating mental states: theory of mind in borderline personality. *Bulletin of the Anna Freud Centre, 12*: 91–115.

Freud, S. (1895 [1950]). Project for a scientific psychology. *S.E., 1*: 283–398. London: Hogarth.

Freud, S. (1900a). *The Interpretation of Dreams. S.E., 4–5.* London: Hogarth.

Freud, S. (1915e). The unconscious. *S.E., 14*: 159–216. London: Hogarth.

Freud, S. (1925h). Negation. *S.E., 19*: 235–242. London: Hogarth.

Freud, S. (1940a [1938]). *An Outline of Psycho-Analysis. S.E., 23*: 141–208. London: Hogarth.

Gabbard, G. O. (1997). A reconsideration of objectivity in the analyst. *International Journal of Psychoanalysis, 78*: 15–27.

Green, A. (1993). *On Private Madness.* Madison, NY: International Universities Press.

Grossman, L. (1996). Psychic reality and psychic testing. *International Journal of Psychoanalysis, 77*: 508–517.

Hoffman, I. Z. (1983). The patient as interpreter of the analyst's experience. *Contemporary Psychoanalysis, 19*: 389–422.

Lear, J. (1993). An interpretation of transference. *International Journal of Psychoanalysis, 74*: 739–755.

Mead, G. H. (1934). *Mind, Self, and Society*, Vol. 1. Chicago, IL: University of Chicago Press.

Mitchell, S. A. (1988). *Relational Concepts in Psychoanalysis, An Integration.* Cambridge, MA: Harvard University Press.

Modell, A. H. (1990). *Other Times, Other Realities*. Cambridge, MA: Harvard University Press.

Nietzsche, F. (1974). *The Gay Science*. W. Kaufman (Trans.). New York: Vintage.

Ogden, T. H. (1994). *Subjects of Analysis*. Hillsdale, NJ: Jason Aronson.

Polanyi, M. (1958). *Personal Knowledge*. Chicago, IL: University of Chicago Press.

Rorty, R. (1979). *Philosophy and the Mirror of Nature*. Princeton, NJ: Princeton University Press.

Rorty, R. (1997). Davidson between Wittgenstein and Tarski (unpublished).

Spezzano, C. (1993). *Affect in Psychoanalysis, A Clinical Synthesis*. Hillsdale, NJ: Jason Aronson.

Stern, D. (1984). *The Interpersonal World of the Infant: A View from Psychoanalysis and Developmental Psychology*. New York: Basic Books.

Stern, D. (1995). *The Motherhood Constellation: A Unified View of Parent–Infant Psychiatry*. New York: Basic Books.

Stolorow, R., & Atwood, G. (1992). *Contexts of Being*. Hillsdale, NJ: Analytic.

Strawson, P. F. (1963). *Individuals, an Essay in Descriptive Metaphysics*. New York: Anchor.

Vygotsky, L. S. (1962). *Thought and Language*. E. Hanfman & G. Vakar (Trans.). Cambridge, MA: MIT.

Wertsch, J. V. (1984). *Vygotsky and the Social Formation of Mind*. Cambridge, MA. Harvard University Press.

Winnicott, D. W. (1971). *Playing and Reality*. New York: Basic Books.

Wittgenstein, L. (1953). *Philosophical Investigations*. G. E. Anscombe (Trans.). Oxford: Blackwell.

Wittgenstein, L. (1972). *On Certainty*. G. E. Anscombe (Trans.). Oxford: Blackwell.

CHAPTER FOUR

Symbols and their function in managing the anxiety of change: an intersubjective approach

James Rose

Introduction

I begin with the idea that the symbolic functioning available to an individual determines the way he or she anticipates and experiences change. I have indicated in my title that I shall take an intersubjective approach to thinking about symbols, so I would like to set out my reasons for bringing in this perspective. The current debate about subjectivity in psychoanalysis begins with the recognition that the encounter in the consulting room is a meeting of two minds. It seems to me that this fact has to be incorporated somehow into an understanding of the process by which a psychoanalyst helps a patient come to know his or her own mind. Goldberg (1998) has suggested that a plethora of different attempts to take on board this fact of the psychoanalytic endeavour have led to an agreement that "the fluidity of the exchange of information in messages between patient and therapist does not allow one to isolate either the one or the other as a fixed point in order to gain access to some reliable set of mental contents" (p. 215). When taken into thinking about the psychoanalytic encounter, there is thus a theoretical conundrum, created by the acceptance of an analyst's subjectivity. If an analyst's perception of reality is open to doubt as a result of the analyst's subjectivity, does psychoanalysis become an impossible profession?

Much of the heat in the current debate on subjectivity seems to derive from the implicit assumption by some that subjectivity implies nothing more than a lack of objectivity. For others, e.g., Renik (1998, p. 487), subjectivity means more than simply not being objective. He argues that to be truly objective, we are forced to accept the fact of the analyst's *irreducible* subjectivity. This looks at first sight to be incorporating an indisputable fact, but it has many logical consequences. For example, we have to ask about the patient's countertransference to the analyst's transference (Atwood & Stolorow, 1984). Indeed, distinguishing whether the analyst's countertransference, an indisputable experiential phenomenon, arises from his lack of objectivity or is the result of a creation within his mind of an aspect of the patient's experience captures precisely the theoretical predicament. It could be one or the other or, maybe, both. Theoretically speaking, they could be sequential or contemporaneous.

In this debate, objectivity becomes as much a problem as subjectivity, to the point where it is almost equated with it. The result is that the protagonists in the debate seem to accuse each other, on the one hand, of being "wild" or, on the other, unreal and positivistic. Ogden's (1986) theory of the "analytic third" arising from the interaction of patient and analyst tries to find a way through the conundrum but possibly does so by altering the sense of what we mean by a subject. His sense seems more akin to the notion of "becoming a subject" Cahn (1998) or, indeed, Lacan's sense of the entry into the symbolic order as defined in his (1945) theory of logical time. In this formulation, we have a theoretical structure that has links with the recognition of dyadic states of consciousness recently postulated by some infant researchers, e.g., Tronick and Weinberg (1997). What makes this possible is that these formulations about what happens between two minds take into account that the interaction is about something other than those two minds themselves.

Marcia Cavell (1998), coming at this problem from the stance of a philosopher, has taken the view that, in order to know our own minds, we require an interaction with another mind in relation to what could be termed objective reality. Without the inclusion of objective reality in a process of what she terms progressive triangulation, she argues that a so-called intersubjective approach collapses into another subjective one. It is this collapse, perhaps, that led Goldberg (1998) to conclude that the new ideas developed by the "inter-subjectivists" were a family of related concepts but with no unifying theory.

In Cavell's analysis of the problem of how we can come to know our own minds, she argues that an implicitly Cartesian notion of subjectivity underpins much psychoanalytic theoretical conceptualization. The sense of this Cartesian notion is that our knowledge of our minds is not connected in any presumable and essential way with the external world, and knowledge of other minds is either impossible or mysterious. If this is how subjectivity is to be defined, it opens it to the kind of attack recently mounted by the intersubjectivists. This is because, in order to avoid the embrace of solipsism, an "objectivity" must be introduced which can be accused of being a positivistic illusion unless it is anchored to something. But the intersubjectivists, she feels, will find themselves in the same position, taking the same risks, but with greater risk of the accusation of "suggestion", if they ignore objective reality.

Renik (1998), as mentioned above, has suggested a "pragmatic" solution to this problem such that the test of the effectiveness of a particular action taken by an analyst is whether it works, i.e., whether it serves to reduce the unhappiness of the patient in the long term. The difficulty with such a pragmatic posture is to determine who decides what is therapeutic; in particular, when such a decision can be made and whether the pragmatic analyst can avoid being in the position of Solomon. This author is in agreement with Cavell's position, but the question then is how to work in accordance with it. An answer, it seems to me, may be found in the observation of the patient's use of the setting as it occurs over time and in the changes of this use. What I seek to do in this chapter is to examine how the essentially subjective (in Cavell's terms) concept of the symbol can be used in an intersubjective way by carefully observing its use, development, and change in the psychoanalytic setting.

The title of this chapter embraces such a broad field of thought that, in order to begin, I need to be specific. There can be few more dramatic changes in one's life than bereavement. The immediately bereaved can feel "in" a state of mind experienced as endless and timeless, whereas an observer, no matter how identified with the bereaved, will be separated from the experience because they will link it with the loss of someone external to the bereaved. The link is not always available to the bereaved because the loss is experienced as a loss of part of the self as well as the loss of someone external. This internal aspect of the experience pervades the self and is bound up with the process of mourning. I have used bereavement as an example of change; and, in thinking about change, I would like to reiterate the notion that all change will involve loss of some kind and, hence, mourning.

In considering change in this way it is easy to become caught in the notion of it somehow implying that, in all cases, there is an ejection from a Garden of Eden. However, a frog is not a tadpole in mourning. We know that change arising from bereavement is likely to be painful, but the arrival of a first child also brings a profound change. Not only has one a child but also one is a parent, and there is a new relationship which influences all other relationships. One's life is instantly more complicated and restructuring and adjustment is necessary. However, we cannot stop there and say simply that some changes are painful whereas others are pleasurable. I think we have to acknowledge the situation as being more complex. This is because, from conception, we may be thought of as systems in dynamic equilibrium with our environment.

This concept we owe to Claude Bernard; i.e., that the organism's prime task is to maintain the integrity of its internal milieu. The infant researchers Tronick and Weinberg (1997) have suggested that Bernard did not appreciate that a critical feature of the homeostatic regulatory process was a dyadic collaborative process (as they put it), which echoes the point made by Cavell. In plainer words, in order to maintain our inner milieu, we deal with other minds. Hence, change presents a challenging duality in that it will threaten a status quo but will need to do so as growth occurs and maturation unfolds. The problem remains whether the anxiety stirred by change mainly concerns loss of the familiar. Laplanche (1997) has suggested that the Copernican-like assault on human narcissism wrought by psychoanalysis is an assault that must be continually mounted because of the persistent temptation to return to the self-centred Ptolemaic outlook. This is brought about by the fact that our body is our outlook, and thus point of view, on the world (so the sun does indeed appear to revolve around us). But he goes further than that by suggesting that change brings with it the threat of the alien unknown. It is this sense of the alien that comes from the awareness of others' minds that we only partially know and the part of our own minds that we do not know: our unconscious. Laplanche therefore puts forward the view that we find this alien other both in the internal and the external world and they support each other. Thus, the unknown other alien mind resonates with and supports the alien-ness of the unconscious.

This means that the two can be potentially blurred and confused, and the choice open to the subject is whether to manage the anxiety of change via the spurious safety of egocentricity or to sacrifice this at the risk of experiencing helplessness with the association of impotence. In the face of these twin dreads, the temptation to return to a self-centred view can be readily understood. To the anxiety stirred by the unknown other alien mind and our own unconscious mind must, of course, be added a third influence: the future, which we can never know in full. The sacrifice of egocentricity permits, of course, the opening of a dialogue with an other mind. We must conclude that the anxiety stirred by change must result from the confrontation with the unknowable as well as with loss.

Having offered some very general thoughts about change and its complexities, I shall now introduce some clinical material related to the case of a patient who came into analysis because he experienced states of mind in which he said he could not stop thinking about headless bodies and a desire to stab. He found these experiences impossible to understand because he felt no affect other than the terror stemming from having such a thought. All concealed spaces, i.e., what he could not know, contained headless bodies that he was about to see. Consciously, he experienced no anger or aggression, but felt himself tormented by what he termed the "ruminations". We might pause here and ask what we mean by "think". It would be truer to the spirit of his description of his state of mind to conceive of his mind being occupied by some things that we could call thoughts. When he experienced these states of mind, he could do little else than be in them and try not to be in them. This presented him with the impossible dilemma of trying not to think about something he was thinking about, which is an impossible task. To try not to think about something is, of course, to think about it, and round and round he went in an obsessive nightmare.

It is clear that, in terms of symptoms, this patient could be diagnosed as an obsessional neurotic, but, it seems to me, the observable phenomena can be thought about in broader terms than diagnosis. The question, to my mind, is whether these symptoms can be thought of as the subject communicating something to the other. It could be said, as part of the initial assessment, that the symptoms created a countertransference pull towards the patient because it was hard not to be become intrigued by these headless bodies and feel drawn towards understanding and interpreting them. Hence, something is projected in the transference that creates a complementary projective counter-identification in the manner described by Grinberg (1962). The question might then be whether the symptomatic thoughts represent something; in other words, have some symbolic significance. However, the emotional appeal experienced in the countertransference represents the analyst's subjectivity. The question is whether the patient's and the analyst's subjectivities will meet through the link partially provided by the symptomatic symbol.

The symbolic content of symptoms was referred to by Freud (1916c) when he suggested that while the hat had been sufficiently well established in the analysis of dreams to be a symbol of the male genital organ, it was not, he thought, an "intelligible one". In order to understand the meaning of the symbol, he suggested that one must find a link between the symbol and the anxiety to which it is related. He referred, in the case of hats, to the tortures that some obsessional patients inflicted upon themselves when they compared the manner in which their friends might doff their hats to them in greeting. From this, they might then impute all kinds of neurotic meanings as to whether a friend might perceive himself as being more important than they, depending on how he doffed his hat. Thus, the anxiety in these instances was castration anxiety; the symptom was in the intertwining of castration anxiety with ordinary social conventions and the communication was in the manner of hat doffing. The hat provided the medium for the expression of the anxiety and thus, in a sense, managed it by enabling it to be expressed in a symbolic form. With this in mind, we are taken immediately to the theory of symbols and their formation and functioning.

Theories of symbols

Laplanche and Pontalis (1973) suggest that, in psychoanalytic thinking, broadly speaking, symbolism refers to any mode of figurative or indirect representation of an unconscious idea. However, there is, they further suggest, a more restricted sense where it is suggested that there is a constancy of the relationship between the symbol and that which is symbolized. This constancy is found not only within an individual but also between them and, to a certain extent, in the mostly widely separated cultures.

Such an assertion of a constancy of relationship is rather unique because, in linguistics, there need be no logical or intrinsic connection between the signifier and the signified. However, the link between the notion of a symbol and language has not been given equal weight by all psychoanalytic theorists. Indeed, I shall argue that psychoanalytic conceptualization of the symbol has tended to concentrate on the symbol as an intrapsychic phenomenon. The effect of this has been that the symbol as an interpsychic medium has been less thought about, with the exception, of course, of Lacan. When I come later to discuss the work of Marcia Cavell, I shall follow, as I understand it, her concept of the difference between the subjective (or the intrapsychic) and the intersubjective.

Psychoanalytic theories of the nature of symbols, and their formation and function, often differ because the phenomena of symbolism are taken as evidence in support of other psychoanalytic concepts. Indeed, it could be said that psychoanalytical understanding of the symbol is largely epi-phenomenal. When a proponent of one outlook criticizes another from another, one gets the impression that the criticism arises from a failure to understand the profound, but unstated, philosophical differences between the proponents, which are separate and distinct from the psychoanalytic differences. In the literature about symbolism and symbolic functioning in psychoanalysis there is, therefore, something of a tower of Babel. However, each theoretical strand offers much, and it is for this reason that I am going to take some space and time to set out my understanding of a number of different approaches. I refer, initially, to three main strands of conceptualization in psycho-analytic theory developed by British thinkers.

First, we may consider the early work of Freud, which was used by Ernest Jones in his 1916 paper, "The theory of symbolism". The paper is a combative one directed at the post-Freudian ex-colleagues of Jones, whom he regarded as revisionists or separatists backing away from Freud's radical views of the human mind. The paper is a virtuoso performance that sets out a psychoanalytic view of the nature of a symbol and the process of symbolization, which it is necessary to keep conceptually separate in our minds. His main thesis is that it is possible to distinguish one fundamental type of indirect representation of one idea by another from other more or less closely allied ones. Consideration of the points of distinction throws light on the nature of indirect figurative representation in general and Jones' view in particular of "true" symbolism.

To distinguish what Jones called "true" symbolism from all other types, he first drew attention to what he saw as the difficulty that is indicated by all forms of symbolism, which concerned the adequate apprehension of affects. In the very broadest sense of the term "symbolism" (which could include metaphor), he felt that it betokened a relative incapacity for either apprehension or commu-nication. This incapacity could be thought of as intellectual or affec-tive in origin, the second of which was much the more important. Further, the mind tends to notice especially those features that interest it because of their resemblance to previous experiences of interest. The appreciation of resemblance facilitates the assimilation of new experience by referring the unknown to the previously known.

In the briefest of summary of his ideas, I quote the following from his paper

All psycho-analytic experience goes to show that the primary ideas of life, the only ones that can be symbolised—those, namely concerning the bodily self, the relation to the family, birth, love and death—retain in the unconscious throughout life their original importance and that from them is derived a very large part of the more secondary interests of the conscious mind. As energy flows from and never to them and as they constitute the most repressed parts of the mind, it is comprehensible that symbolism takes place in one way only. Only what is repressed is symbolised (in the true sense): only what is repressed needs to be symbolised. This conclusion is the touchstone of the psycho-analytic theory of symbolism. [p. 116]

Here we see Jones drawing directly on the topographical model of the mind developed by Freud arising from his work on dreams and their interpretation. It will be recalled that Freud saw dreams as the expression of unconscious wishes that had to be disguised in order to preserve sleep because the wishes would disturb sleep if they were allowed into consciousness. In 1915 he wrote about repression, saying that "The essence of repression lies simply in turning something away and keeping it at a distance from consciousness" (1915e). The distinction he later made between thing presentation and word presentation in "The unconscious" (1915e) anticipates a development away from the repression model of symbolization. Its significance is that it enables us to see that the kinds of symbolization available affect not simply the availability of particular experiences (which have been repressed) but also concern the very possibilities of thought and experience. Thus, he proposed a notion of *agnosia* (implying something which cannot be known) in addition to *aphasia* (that for which there is no word).

Of particular note is Jones' thought that symbolism betokened an incapacity to communicate. Perhaps one of the most irksome ideas is that of the idea of a "true" symbol, which is an epiphenomenon of repression. Precisely because it is taken to be evidence of repression, it means that something is kept from consciousness, and yet something about this "unintelligibility" draws attention to itself and, hence, communicates. As we have seen above, my patient's preoccupation with unintelligible headless bodies inevitably draws our attention. It may appear odd that Jones made so little reference to language, particularly as symbolic phenomena are associated with language and it was in linguistics that much conceptualization about symbolic phenomena had been developed. But Jones was concerned with what he considered the "true" symbol in the psychoanalytic sense. Jones' priority, at the time, was to make Freudian psychoanalytic thinking distinct by demonstrating the unconscious, which had political as well as scientific purpose. As a result, it can be concluded that Jones' conception of symbolism was essentially a subjective rather than an intersubjective one.

Nevertheless, returning to the patient mentioned earlier, with these ideas in mind, we might be led to wonder what repressed ideas the headless bodies represent, why they have to be repressed, and what they prevent from being known. This leads to the relationship between the symbol and the symbolizer. The next theoretical development I wish to consider is that deriving from Klein and its development by Segal (1957) through her distinction between symbolic equation and symbolic representation. Segal illustrated this difference by comparing two male patients. One was a musician who, when asked why he no longer played his violin, replied with indignation whether the enquirer wished him to masturbate in public. In other words, the violin was, in effect, *equated* with the penis, and in an extremely concrete way. The other, also a musician, reported a dream in which he and a young girl were playing a violin duet. He had associations to the dream of fiddling and masturbating, from which it emerged that the violin represented his genital and playing the violin represented a masturbation phantasy of sexual intercourse with the girl. We can see that in this case the violin acts as a *representative* and is not *equated* in the same concrete way. The two kinds of symbol are, of course, epiphenomenal of the depressive and the paranoid–schizoid positions, respectively. Thus, Segal (1957) says:

> Not only the actual content of the symbol but the very way in which symbols are formed and used seems to reflect precisely the ego's state of development and its ways of dealing with its objects . . .

and, in addition, that

> symbol formation is an activity of the ego attempting to deal with the anxieties stirred by its relation to the object and is generated primarily by the fear of bad objects and the fear of the loss or inaccessibility of good objects. [p. 392]

What I wish to emphasize is the difference between the situation in which separateness is difficult, if not impossible, *as is implied by the symbolic equation,* and where it is possible to separate out oneself from others and retain the separateness of different experiences in relation to the same other, *as is implied by the symbolic representation*. Symbolic equation is to be still lost in the immediacy of a moment in a potentially persecutory way. Symbolic representation enables the symbolizer to be separate from the symbol and symbolized. Hence, we can see two different possible ways in which the symbolizer mediates his experience through a symbol, each with their psychic advantages and drawbacks.

There is, however, a difficulty in making fear or loss the essential drivers of symbolism, because it precludes the possibility of symbols representing the creation of something new emerging from unconscious processes in response to demand for change. In essence, my idea is that the complexity created by unknowable nothingness, or an absence of being, stimulates symbolization as much as the threat of the bad or the loss of the good. It is equally true that the representative symbol permits the embrace of complexity because of the triangulation of symbol, symbolized, and symbolizer. This embrace of complexity the symbolic equation cannot fulfil and seeks to obviate or avoid.

The theory of symbolization in a representational sense is especially useful for understanding mourning and the pathologies of mourning. A capacity for symbolization in a representational sense means that the pleasurable aspects of the lost object can be distinguished from the unpleasurable and internalized into the self, which feels enhanced as a result. When symbolization is on the basis of equations, loss can only be felt as a persecution. The bereaved is stuck with their pain and cannot find relief. The difference between these two positions is that the symbolic equation creates a situation in which the symbol is indistinguishable from the self whereas in the representation something separate is possible. This means that it is possible to think with the representative in a manner different from the equation. This arises from the difference between the equation and the representation resting on the degree of projective identification utilized by the individual. We might say, for example, that in the symbolic equation described above, there is an equation of the meaning of words because there is a massive projective identification between the musician's penis (as an internal part object) and his violin. So far as this musician is concerned, there is therefore apparently no difference in reality between playing his violin and masturbating in public.

However, as listeners to the account, we might wonder whether the questioner is having his leg pulled or whether he is being seen by the musician as someone who is asking the musician to humiliate himself. In other words, the meaning of the musician's reply depends on its context. This idea of context relates to the notion of *triangulation* of symbol, symbolized, and symbolizer. In essence, this enables the possibility of assessing the relationship between two elements relative to the context created by a third. The link with the notion of progressive triangulation introduced earlier seems obvious, and the triangular space suggested by the symbolic representation offers a model of the embrace of complexity by allowing increasing elaboration of this triangular space over time. At any one point of time, it means that a relationship can be placed in a context that in turn means that the meaning of this relationship can be assessed in a way that is impossible without any kind of contextual referent.

In principle, there is no contextual referent in a pure symbolic equation; hence, the equation seems quite "real" and subjectively indisputable. In the symbolic representation, the presence of the context dissolves this concrete equation. The result is that meaning, and its elaboration, becomes a possibility. It must be said, however, that probably the symbolic equation hardly ever exists in pure form. There is always a context, even though it may be that, in an analysis, it is the analyst's task to provide and then identify a context so that what are meaningless symbolic equations to an analysand can become symbolic representations. Hence, the analyst provides the means of triangulation, where necessary. Indeed, this may be a major function of interpretation and creates the space to think.

The symbol of the headless body

Returning to the man who could not easily shake the ideas of headless bodies out of his mind, two features stood out from the beginning in the pattern of his feelings and ideation. First, it seemed that there was some kind of representation here but what was represented remained unconscious. The patient had no conscious means of interpreting the meaning of his ideas but felt enveloped in them.

Indeed, at times he lived in them and was unable to escape these characteristics of a symbolic equation.

Second, whereas I could feel a strong temptation to try to interpret these ideas, I noted a strong resistance on his part to any efforts of this kind, even though he kept talking about his thoughts. This interesting feature brings forward two aspects of the word symbol in its derivation from Greek. In one sense, as pointed out by Wright (1991), it means a throwing together of things (*Symballein*) but it also derives from the Greek *symbolon*. This denotes the division into two of a recognizable something that was used as a means of recognition by members of forbidden religious groups. By the means of joining the fragments together, Wright brought this etymology to attention as a means of showing how the symbol (or fragment) betrayed the separation of symbol from symbolized. This he linked to Freud's theory of repression concerning the separation of thing presentations from word presentations. It illustrates an interesting duality about symbols in that they can both represent and hide, and that can be part of their intention. There was the possibility that, however much my patient felt persecuted by these ideas, he seemed, paradoxically, not to wish to be separated from them.

Therefore, this man wanted not to think these ideas but he could not stop. The compulsion suggested that there was something very powerful or painful associated with, and hidden by, these ideas, and this was the only way they could be mentally accommodated. If we combine the theoretical views we have so far, we can say that something is being repressed and that, whatever this is, our patient is extremely reluctant to give up something about it. Furthermore, this seemed to be a very active process. It seemed that I must accept that there would be a lot of resistance towards me if I were seen as desiring to bring these somethings, whatever they were, to consciousness. This takes us to the nature of the relationships in which this man found himself, or, in other words, the context of the symbol.

In treating this man, I noticed the things described below.

1. He experienced onsets of these thoughts intermittently. They seemed to start when there was a sense of loss or disillusionment with someone important to him but they seemed to recede and indeed disappear after there had been some

emotional contact with me. When I made an interpretive link between their onset and his loss of contact with me, it met at the beginning with steadfast denial. On the other hand, the interpretation of their disappearance in relation to emotional contact with me did not meet the same fate.

2.   The thoughts were experienced as coming from outside him.

3.   There seemed to be an experience of me as someone who was a detective seeking to discover something for which he should feel guilty and should be condemned.

4.   The thoughts became very powerful when there was a conscious realization of approaching separation and permanent loss.

As a general observation of him, it seemed that here were three typical reactions to the prospect of separation. The first was to deny its importance: that is, to seek to obliterate any sense of the importance of the loss and any emotional reactions to it or, indeed, any sense of pain. The second was to cut himself off from the experience as if to deny that it ever happened. The third was to suffer powerful onsets of the thoughts that represented a need to fall ill. It was clear that, despite the denial, the prospect of separation at some level provoked terrible anxiety. There was a fear of being destroyed and the response was in part to destroy that which had created such anxiety. In addition, there seemed to be a possibility that, in the process of falling ill, there was a phantasy of regaining what had been lost. Once the "unintelligible" symptomatic symbol of the headless body was linked to the experience of separation, it seemed to me that the symbol began to acquire some meaning. Separation provided a context in which what the symbol represented could emerge. We may, therefore, hypothesize that a symbol hides when the context is removed, ignored, or denied.

Separation and the headless body

To substantiate my hypothesis that this patient's symptomatic symbol had been unconsciously created as a refuge into which he could withdraw when faced with the prospect of separation, I offer the following clinical material after some years of his analysis. This patient was treated in the London Clinic of Psychoanalysis. For patients treated in the London Clinic under its subsidized scheme, there was at the time an initial limit of three years, which could be extended in certain cases. I obtained an extension of one year. At the beginning of this fourth year we had begun in the knowledge that, so far as the Clinic was concerned, there was a known termination date. This did not necessarily mean the analysis would end, if he and I chose not to end it, but it would no longer be under the auspices of the London Clinic. I made this clear to him as we began in September.

He reacted as if he was determined not to think about it and continued on in his timeless way until the approach of the Easter break. Then, when he returned, there were signs that the prospect of a real ending was starting to become conscious. There came a day when he asked what would happen in the autumn after the analysis had ended. In other words, he was assuming, despite what I had said, that I would end his analysis. This session gradually ushered in a powerful onset of the ruminations. I will describe a session during this period.

This session took place on a Tuesday. On the day before, he had reported a dream, which was not that common for him to do. In the dream, he was lying on the couch in the consulting room but he was facing the opposite way round. I was behind him and moved my leg so that it rubbed against his. He was embarrassed in telling me this dream because of what he considered was the homosexual content; that is, he felt that he was telling me that he thought I was homosexual. Being conscious that this was a dream told on a Monday, that there were signs of reversal in the dream and that the prospect of ending hung over us like the sword of Damocles, I had the impression that this dream contained an anxiety even more fearful for him than telling me I was "queer", as he put it. I interpreted that what was consciously felt in the dream as my approach to him was a means of reversing a situation in which he felt I abandoned him, leaving him feeling as helpless as he felt in the dream.

He replied to this by telling me that he always wore brown shoes in contrast to his father, who always wore black ones. This brought to my mind an oft-repeated memory of his father coming to his bedroom and touching him through the bedclothes, resting his hand "on top of my dick". In telling this story, he had often left me with the question in my mind of whether he was talking about an abuse or whether he resisted his own affectionate feelings of love towards his father by transforming them into a homosexual approach. By telling me about the colour of his shoes, I felt I was his father in the transference and that somewhere he feared a sexual approach. However, his embarrassment, rather than anxiety, at telling the dream suggested to me that it was not at all like that. I thought he might be embarrassed at his affectionate feelings towards me and I told him so. In addition, I said that he found analysis sometimes very dangerous because it could be that I held up a mirror to him and showed him something horrifying that was derived from the strength of his needs for what he experienced me as being. This was followed the next day by this session.

The session began by the patient saying that it was as if no time had elapsed between when he had left the day before and when he had arrived that day. His ruminations had been going full blast. Being mindful of how he seemed to have attacked the sense of separation by replacing it with the ruminations, I took this up with him by wondering why it was no time seemed to have elapsed when, of course, it had. This met with an irritated response as if to say why wasn't I interested in his illness. Despite these protestations, I persisted in taking this up because I knew from work in previous sessions that there was something about separation that he found very disturbing. He replied that he was always like that. He wiped things out when he left, but he added that suffering the ruminations seemed to pull people towards him. I said that perhaps his mind was full of ruminations to pull me towards him and to make sure that I would not send him away at the end of the session without having something about which to feel guilty. This led him to observe at some length that he could always fall ill to get out of things and when he thought people were angry with him.

I chose to intervene in his discursive review of his past by wondering aloud what it was that had been going on between us that he got out of by being ill. I did this because I was wondering whether separation, at the unconscious level, initially produced anger at being displaced but was experienced, at the conscious level, as anxiety at the prospect of being seen as angry. By interpreting the possibility of displacement of immediate anxieties into the past, I felt we might get closer to angrier feelings that his review of the past seemed designed to avoid.

After some skirmishing, he expressed his view that I saw him as a "little fuck" who couldn't do without analysis and he hated me for regarding him as contemptibly dependent. This seemed to be nearer to the anger that I had suspected, but which he seemed to be so afraid to express because of his fear of the consequences. This enabled us to explore his feelings and reactions at the end of a session when I said it was time. He acknowledged that his rage vanished into ruminations that hid his anger with me and his fear of me, which resulted from the anger, in a single destructive cut. Once in the ruminations he was ill and immune from the painful feeling arising from separation. However, the violence of the severance meant that the experience in the *après coup* was void.

Symbols as creations

What I now wish to examine is the link between the experience of change arising from the experience of separation and the various ways in which the symbol of the headless body seems to manage the anxiety associated with these changes. To pursue this, I will turn to a third strand of psychoanalytic theory: Winnicott's theory of transitional objects and transitional spaces, because of its intersubjective conception of the genesis and development of a symbol that includes a temporal dimension.

At the heart of Winnicott's theory (1945) about the infant's experience in the early months of life is the notion of illusion. He envisaged the newborn infant as being like an organism without a skin to separate and protect it from the physical environment. In the early months, Winnicott said that the mother must enable the baby to maintain a sense of what he called omnipotence. Winnicott's use of the word in this context refers to the infant's system of thought being based entirely on wish fulfilment or primary process thinking; e.g., "I want it to be so and it is so". He is not referring to a defence.

At the beginning, its mother has to act as a skin for the infant. The mother, by an almost total adaptation to the infant's needs, affords the infant the opportunity for the illusion that her breast is part of the infant. It is, as it were, under the baby's magical control. As Winnicott put it,

> omnipotence is nearly a fact of experience. In another language, the breast is created by the infant over and over again out of the infants capacity for love or (one can say) out of need. A subjective phenomenon develops in the baby which we call the mother's breast. The

mother places the actual breast just where the infant is ready to create and at the right moment. [1953, p. 90]

Winnicott believed that the mother's eventual task is gradually to disillusion the infant, but that she had no hope of success unless at first she had been able to give sufficient opportunity for illusion. If the mother failed in this task, a premature shattering of the omnipotence may occur, meaning that the baby had to turn its attention to external objects prematurely and conform to them, thereby creating a compliant false self. If things proceeded well enough, the infant would be able to tolerate increasing degrees of separation from mother. Thus, in his view, a *space* develops between mother and infant. The nature of this space and its perception and use is of central interest to us.

Winnicott (1951) took the view that, while psychoanalysis had established beyond doubt the need to distinguish between internal and external reality, there was a need to define what he called "the third part of the life of a human being". This was:

> an intermediate area of experiencing, to which inner reality and external life both contribute. It is an area that is not challenged because no claim is made on its behalf except that it shall exist as a resting place for the individual engaged in the perpetual human task of keeping inner and outer reality separate yet interrelated. [p. 90]

It will be clear that, within the infant's omnipotence, all objects will be perceived as part of the infant. There is no such thing, therefore, as a "not-me" object. Gradual separation from the mother and the accompanying process of disillusionment introduces the idea of objects outside omnipotence; while these objects are experienced within the intermediate space of experience described above, they will be experienced as "not me" objects but it will not be clear whether they are outside omnipotent control or not. It is common to observe that infants latch on to a something that is clearly evaluated by the infant more highly than others. What will be clear to the infant's parents will be the special relationship that their infant has to this object—otherwise known as a transitional object. The transitional object may be called by we adults the teddy bear, or a bit of blanket, but to so regard this object as such with the adult mind is to risk missing the point.

If we define the transitional object as the infant's teddy bear and put it away in our mental toy cupboard, we will lose sight of the importance of the area of experiencing or the developing transitional space in which the transitional object is situated. For the infant, the development of this space and the manipulation of objects within it, permits the experience of becoming aware of the difference between inner and outer reality and the limits on omnipotence. Where we find, in an adult, evidence of a means by which this distinction is blurred or obviated, then we may hypothesize that for some reason the subject has sought to retain omnipotent control over something against all the evidence.

Transitional phenomena and the management of anxiety

In the case described above, it seemed that the anxiety that the patient sought to manage was separation anxiety. However, consciously acknowledging separation anxiety turned him, in his own mind, into a dependent "little fuck", which was a crippling narcissistic wound. He told me that a customary response to difficult situations at school had been to go to the sick room, but this had been at considerable cost to his self esteem. When he grew into an adult in an adult body, a new "sick room" or refuge had to be created, and the headless body ideas emerged during adolescence. In the work of analysis it became possible to identify a number of themes condensed into the idea of the headless body.

The first of these was that they contained a sense of himself cut off from his object. All separation was experienced by him as a cut. Second, his retaliatory response of cutting himself off from those who left him and obliterating any trace of their effects could also be detected. This was revealed in the analysis by his reaction at the end of a session in which he could wipe it from his mind. Third, the sense of murderousness implied by this obliteration not only destroyed what it was that caused him psychic pain but also gave him a powerful sense of his violent strength. This had to be kept quite secret for fear of retaliation by others if they found out the "truth" about him. This led directly to the sense of his analyst being experienced as a detective. Finally, the ideas would easily provide a sense for himself and others that he was ill (which, of course, he was).

Presented like this, it is easy to wonder why this man came into analysis at all, because the secondary gains from his symptoms were as great as they were. But, somewhere, he was aware of how crippled he was because he deprived himself of the rewards of relationships in order to seek an unending relationship in which separation from his object of desire never occurred. With this patient, insight only came when, after long and careful attention to his reactions to separations, there was a realization that the violence contained by his symptomatic symbol stemmed from the violence of his reaction to loss. He had, therefore, created a symbol to deal with the intolerable experience of loss—intolerable because of the desire for total control—but had then become lost in it. He lived almost symbiotically in his symbol and could only separate from it and look at it through analysis. When he saw the headless body as his own creation as a response to the prospect of change, which eventually he did, he began to separate from it and see why he had created it. He could then see that for all its gratifying illusions, it actually was self defeating. The effectiveness of this analysis was revealed by the fact that when some years later he went through a tumultuous series of changes in his life which he partly initiated, but to which he also had to respond, there was no return of the obsessive ruminatory thoughts, which astonished him.

When asking whether these headless bodies are symbols, I think it is important to consider how this patient used these ideas in a communicative way with others and, therefore, in the transference. The question, thus, is not whether they are symbols but *how they can become symbolic*. With his ruminations in his mind he was ill, and could not be expected to do anything. He compared them, at the outset of his analysis, to spectacles or glasses, i.e., "you don't hit a man with glasses on". Because the ruminations had been experienced as coming from outside him, they rendered him in his consciousness of himself as mild and inoffensive. Paradoxically, they were revealed to him by analysis to be full of aggressive intent, but this could only happen when the symptom was seen in the context of separation. This betrays the subject's unconscious desire to the other and provides the means of undoing the riddle of the repression, which by its nature will not give up its secret willingly.

This is particularly the case where the symbol is expressive of a desire for a retreat from change and thus may be thought of as antagonistic to change.

Winnicott's work tries to capture the significance of symbols in the creation of experience. In relating the transitional object to symbolism, Winnicott said that whereas we could understand the nature of transitional objects while not fully understanding the nature of symbolism, symbolism could only be properly studied in the process of the growth of the individual. What is reflected by these thoughts is Winnicott's concern with the use and function of the transitional object. This gives us a model that enables us to think about how the individual uses a symbol and why this active and creative process functions in the way it seems. A symbol, as a transitional phenomenon, therefore, can be thought of as a creation linking psychic reality with external reality and unconsciously using it in the discourse with the other. We can, therefore, observe the progressive triangulation postulated by Cavell through the link between the use of the symbol and its entwining with external, material reality. This permits a symptom to become symbolic and thereby communicative, because seeing the symptom in the context of the setting enables it to become a symbol.

The question remains as to why it is created, to which the answer could be that the only alternative is to remain in egocentric subjective isolation. The crucial point is the entry of external reality and its use in response to the thoughts or actions of (m)other'(s) minds. This separates Winnicott's transitional object from Jones' and Segal's conceptualizations of the symbol. The second feature that distinguishes these ideas is that the transitional object develops over time, which brings in the dimension of historicity. We can see a comparable analysis by Lacan in his thoughts about the "fort da" game, which brought together the notions of temporality and the development of the symbolic order.

It is with respect to this *temporal* aspect that I wish to contrast the patient discussed above with my next patient, who did not bring a symptom expressed in a symbol but who developed one in the course of an analysis. When this was analysed, it revealed a possibility that this was not evidence of something that had been repressed, but of something that was being de-repressed. My evidence for this contention is that it was hard to see how the

particular development of this analysis could be much other than
the recommencement of a normal process of development that had
been arrested during latency. It seemed, therefore, to be evidence of
a fixation that was opened up by the creation of a symbol which
provided the communication to the analyst of showing the way the
analysis would develop and also the anxieties that would be
aroused. It is because it developed in the course of the analysis that
I regard this case as an example showing the *temporal* aspect in the
way it demonstrably developed and changed.

A symbol as a creative response

When my second patient came into analysis, there were two
features about her history and presentation that stood out from the
beginning. First, she had been abandoned at about the age of five
by her mother, who left her husband (my patient's father) to care
for their three daughters, of whom my patient was the eldest. The
second feature was that, despite being in a stable relationship and
having a determination for a baby, she had very little idea of the
impact that becoming a mother would have on her life.

From the outset, this patient was very concerned about the
boundaries of the setting. She always arrived precisely on time and
was intolerant of even the slightest overrun by a minute of the
session. She paid punctiliously on time and yet she refused to use
the couch. It was clear that she could envisage herself on the couch,
but could not bring herself to lie on it. This reflected the quality of
the analysis in this period, which was not one characterized by an
easy ability to free associate. The refusal to use the couch could not
but arouse a curiosity in me, because here was a woman who
wished to have an analysis but acted in such a way as to impede
substantially its efficacy. In view of her history, it seemed to me that
despite my curiosity it was important to wait until the meaning
became clear. At that point, I hypothesized that the apparent phobia
was a reaction to being alone in the consulting room with a male
analyst, which clearly might well have something to do with being
left with her father on her mother's departure.

She became pregnant and gave birth to a daughter to whom she
was devoted. For the next year, she attended her analysis with her

daughter and the analysis turned in many ways on her anxieties of being able to be a good mother. She was extremely reluctant to leave her daughter in the care of someone else when she came to analysis, which, on the face of it, seemed to be a refusal to be the rejecting and abandoning mother that she had in her mind. When she began to attend on her own once more, she became more determined to use the couch. But she would sit on it, or sit on the floor with it at her back, and feel very self-conscious. It soon became apparent that to enable her to actually lie on it required an interpretation of the anxieties giving rise to her self-consciousness. After a short period, during which she became progressively less phobic of the couch, there developed an intensely erotic transference. It was as though she was finally able to be a woman in the room and let the analysis penetrate her mind.

I bring this case because it seems that the phobia of the couch and the analysis represented both her conscious fear of her male analyst and, more particularly, her unconscious desires and her fear of her analyst's reaction. She was, as it were, reliving her experience of being left with her father by her mother but this time through the medium of being in possession of a fully mature female sexual body. While this did have a psychotic quality in that it was experienced so concretely, despite the obvious hostile possibilities, it seemed to me that it concerned more her final acquisition of her woman's sexual body for herself. In this case, it seemed to be clear that the erotization of the transference was not a resistance to the analysis and that it would have been incorrect to interpret it as such.

There are two aspects that deserve emphasis. The first is that the phobia represented the repression of sexual desires. However, the choice of the focus of the phobia (the couch) and her deliberate seeking of a male analyst (i.e., with a couch) represented an unconscious drive to realize her sexual self as a woman. In her process of selecting me, she had seen two men and, at the outset of the analysis, told me that she had rejected the other because he had looked at her breasts in an unwelcome way. After some years, however, she stated that the truth was that she hadn't found him sexually attractive. I doubt that this "truth" had been available to her at the time. Hence, we see a pre-conscious creative drive for change in the presence of the defence against the original difficulty. The refusal to use the couch provides the cue to activate the analyst's subjectivity in the countertransference. The couch, which was the focus of the phobia in consciousness, was also the unconscious goal, which was to realize her sexual self in union with the male analyst. Hence, what was initially "I couldn't lie on the couch" became "I want to lie on the couch with you" as her psychic centre of gravity moved from her self-consciousness to her drives and hence from preoccupation with the other mind (i.e., the analyst) to thinking about her own mind.

Symbols and change

My purpose in recounting some aspects of these analyses has been to point to some links between the inevitable anxiety of change and symbols that have been brought to, or are created in the course of, an analysis as a response to it. These, then, bring a meaning to the change and eventually reveal, through their examination in the context of the analytic dialogue over time, the manner in which the patient in the first case developed a psychic retreat and, in the case of the second, sought to undo a fixation that had created a developmental arrest. When I use the word "meaning" above, I am emphasizing the possibilities for the analyst to use the emergence of a symbol *as a means of helping the patient triangulate and thereby separate the conscious content of the symbol from its unconscious meaning, which can then be communicated.* This means listening for what the patient is unconsciously saying to the analyst, which can be done if we allow the psychoanalytic process to create a context for the symptom as it presents itself. The first patient says to his analyst that he cannot bear to be separated from his analyst; the second says that she wishes her mind to be penetrated by her analyst and/but she cannot distinguish her mind from her body.

A useful criterion, therefore, for thinking about these different types of meaning concerns the opportunities offered by a symbol for the symbolizer to stand outside the situation he or she is in and to understand what is happening. We could call this *the opportunities for triangulation* offered by a symbol. The symbol described in the first case above did not allow this, and indeed this was its very purpose. The symbol in the second case can more accurately be said to have developed in response to the setting. It provided the means to stand outside the situation because it provoked the self-consciousness that it did. Hence, it is perhaps more helpful to consider the opportunities for triangulation offered by symbols than to try to identify and systematically interrelate different kinds of symbols.

Does a symbol represent or present?

In an analysis, there is a development of a language between patient and analyst about the patient's inner world for which, before the analysis, there were no words: a kind of *aphasia*. We can see in the case of both, but particularly my second patient, that this was preceded by a phase of *agnosia*: a period during which something was not be allowed to be known. This suggests that pre-conscious activity is an essential component of symbol formation and functioning.

To begin to think about this issue, I have found it helpful to use Susanne Langer's (1942) concepts of *presentational* and *discursive* symbolism. In short, she considered that *presentational symbols* developed in artistic reaction expressed as a mode of symbolic activity, with its own rules and rigour, as has verbal language, but with a different purpose. The purpose of presentational symbols was to present the patterns of our emotional and experiential life in an evocative and sensual way. Their purpose was not primarily to present ideas as propositions, which was the role of language, but to show the nature of the patterns in which we live and the experiences we have. In other words, they are the means by which we can come to know something before we are sure we know it, and they precede a communicative capability. The *discursive symbolism* of language, on the other hand, conveyed relations and discriminations in the world of objects through an agreed set of conventional symbols that merely referred to but did not iconically or imagistically present that which they symbolized.

At this point, we have arrived at the idea that a symbol that develops in the course of an analysis or is brought for analysis must be seen as part, and in the context, of the discourse between patient and analyst. The symbols used or developed in the discourse will inevitably have discursive and presentational aspects. At the outset, the presentational aspects will inevitably be far more in evidence. Although it may not be immediately apparent to either analyst or analysand what the meaning of a symbol is, it can become more discursive given time and effort. This takes us to the work of Lacan, because he is concerned with the development of subjectivity over time.

Lacan's significance in psychoanalytical thinking is growing, partly as a result of the increasing interest in intersubjectivity in psychoanalysis. Part of the difficulty that the Anglo-Saxon world has had in understanding him stems from his determination to look at Freud from a different philosophical standpoint, which, at its heart, challenges the notion of the conscious ego being the subject. This exalts the concept of the ego, which was, in his view, simply a phenomenon of the (in his terms) Imaginary order. In essence, this conception of the subject was, in Lacan's view, the legacy of Descartes (see Lacan, 1988). It is debatable whether the consequences of this implicit assumption has bedevilled the development of psychoanalytic theory since the dominant language of psychoanalysis ceased to be German and became English.

In her paper referred to above, Marcia Cavell (1998), without making reference to Lacan but, I think, essentially agreeing with him, also disputed the Cartesian view that our knowledge of our minds is not connected in any essential way with the external world and that knowledge of other minds is either impossible or mysterious. Although it could be said, she thinks, that, with Descartes, subjectivity in its modern sense is born and has much common sense appeal, it does now seem that there are insuperable problems created by such a limited view. Cavell points out that Freud unquestioningly accepted the Cartesian ocular view of self-knowledge. For example, he says about psychical reality that it "is as much unknown to us as the reality of the external world, and is as incompletely presented by the data of consciousness as is the external world by the communication of our sense organs" (1900a, p. 613).

One of the principal difficulties with the Cartesian subject is that it does not make room for historicity. We, Cavell says, are now inclined to think that knowledge is never certain and it grows not by transcending partiality but through a dialogue over time. This idea of dialogue immediately implies that intersubjectivity is what is important to consider in the development of a theory of mind and, by implication, a theory of symbolism once the communicative or discursive aspects of symbols are given their proper place.

As I have said earlier, the significance of her dispute of the Cartesian view for psychoanalysts lies in the test to which some psychoanalytical theoretical assumptions are put by implication. In essence, Cavell's viewpoint is that subjectivity goes hand in hand with intersubjectivity. As discussed above, an intersubjectivity that separates itself from considerations of objectivity and intersubjectively verifiable truth is no intersubjectivity at all, but collapses into a subjectivity. As we have seen, the objective features of the psychoanalytical setting can provide the cues and hooks for the subjectivities of the patient and the analyst to find one another. In the first case, it was the nature of symptomatic symbol that aroused the analyst's attention and in the second it was the refusal to use the couch. But such a search takes time, which is a crucial feature of the objectivity of the psychoanalytic setting. Given time, the original cue takes on a meaning in the context of the objective setting.

A crucial aspect of the psychoanalytical process, which links it with the objective world, is its temporality, which links with the idea of historicity mentioned above. This is, of course, central to the understanding of Lacan's theory of the symbolic order and why he regarded the central importance of Freud's paper *Beyond the Pleasure Principle* (1920g) to be its introduction of the notion of temporality. I think that the objectivity of time is what also provides an essential point of triangulation in the model proposed by Cavell, and so there begins to be a convergence of her views with those of Lacan. Not least in this convergence is the idea that subjectivity grows out of intersubjectivity and not the other way round.

What we have observed in the two cases described above is a process in which a patient and analyst could come to understand something centrally important to the patient through seeing how an aspect of the objective, and indisputable, psychoanalytic setting was used by the patient to communicate something about the anxieties that brought them to analysis in the first place. In the first case, it was the fact of the end of the session and the ending of an analysis that was the objective feature; in the second, it was the fact of the couch. This objective feature, on the one hand, acted as a means of focusing the expression of the patient's anxiety in the transference situation and, on the other, provided the means of communication from patient to analyst about this anxiety by enabling it to be lived out in the relationship. Now this perspective, in both cases, was not immediately apparent, but became apparent through a dialogue between patient and analyst over time. Hence, the significance of the symbols moved from the presentational to the communicative to the subjectively meaningful.

To my mind, the psychoanalytic theory of symbolism becomes of especial interest because of Cavell's views on *triangulation* as a means by which we can come to know our own minds. It enables us to develop a model that will account for the clinical phenomena observed above. This will also perhaps enable psychoanalysts to develop their own theory of symbolic phenomena rather than trying to incorporate non-psychoanalytic concepts of symbolism by fitting them into a psychoanalytic theoretical rubric, which inevitably creaks. The great theoretical and technical promise offered by a better understanding of symbolic phenomena in the psychoanalytic setting and discourse may be that it will provide a means of understanding of how to open egocentric closed systems. To do this, we need to develop the notion of triangulation and add a temporal dimension to the concept—thus creating a concept of *progressive triangulation*.

Conclusion

To conclude and summarize, my objective in this chapter has been to explore the idea that understanding the process of symbolization available to an individual will help us to understand the way in which they experience changes and manage the inevitable anxiety of the pressure for change. The anxiety of change is always with us and is the consequence of the fact that we only partially know the future, our own minds, or the mind of the other. The choice open to the subject is to retreat into Ptolemaic egocentricity or to engage with the world and others. In the egocentric position, the mind reacts to an experience of *agnosia* by finding a means of *presenting* to the subject the nature of their anxiety, but this may not be necessarily intelligible. At this point, a symbol's function can be both to reveal and to hide (*symballein/symbolon*) and may prove difficult to distinguish from a symptom. From this, the symbol can come to equate to, and be, a psychic retreat (Steiner, 1993). Alternatively, the subject can break out of the egocentric position and use this presentation as a means of managing the anxiety more creatively by communicating the anxiety to others *discursively*. To do this a context for a symbol must be found, and it can then become representative and communicative. It is in the interaction of the subject with others that the symbol can become meaningful, which is the third stage of managing the anxiety of change. The management of anxiety in any system involves relating that system's internal and external worlds, either to connect or divide them. I propose that symbols in their formation function in the manner described above to manage the inevitable anxiety of change.

We seem to have arrived at a position of recognizing not only the subjective significance of symbols but also their, perhaps original, intersubjective significance. Thus, we seem to conclude that symbols are not only about repression or loss but also about the management of the anxiety of change and the opening or closing of discourse with other minds. Whereas they do reflect the relationship between the individual and his/her objects, above all they reflect an individual's response to the inevitability of the demand for change created simply because we are alive. They also link the demands of psychic reality to the strictures and exigencies of external reality. In the process of change they will develop and contain the hopes and fears of the central actor in the process, whether trapping them in a retreat or facilitating a creative response. It is my contention that, by seeing and responding to symbols in their intersubjective context rather than thinking of them as purely subjective phenomena, we can make greater progress in understanding our patients and helping them to emerge from their psychic retreats, if they so wish.

References

Atwood G., & Stolorow, R. D. (1984). *Structures of Subjectivity: Explorations in Psychoanalytic Phenomenology*. Hillsdale, NJ: Analytic Press.

Cavell, M. (1998). Triangulation, one's own mind and objectivity. *International Journal of Psychoanalysis, 79*: 449–467.

Cahn, R. (1998). The process of becoming a subject in adolescence. In: M. Perret-Catipovic & F. Ladame (Eds.), *Adolescence and Psycho-analysis* (pp. 149–160) London: Karnac.

Freud, S. (1900a). *The Interpretation of Dreams. S.E.,* 4–5. London: Hogarth.

Freud, S. (1915e). The unconscious. *S.E., 14:* 159–208. London: Hogarth.

Freud, S. (1916c). A connection between a symbol and a symptom. *S.E., 14:* 339–340. London: Hogarth.

Freud, S. (1920g). *Beyond the Pleasure Principle. S.E., 18:* 7–64. London: Hogarth.

Goldberg, A. (1998). Deconstructing the dialectic. *International Journal of Psychoanalysis, 79:* 215–228.

Grinberg, L. (1962). On a specific aspect of counter-transference due to the patient's projective identification. *International Journal of Psychoanalysis, 43:* 436–440.

Jones, E. (1916). The theory of symbolism. In: E. Jones (Ed.), *Papers on Psycho-Analysis* (pp. 87–146). London: Maresfield Reprints.

Lacan, J. (1945). Le temps logique et l'assertion de certitude anticipée. In: *Ecrits.* Paris: Edition de Seuil, 1966. Translated in *The Newsletter of the Freudian Field,* 2(2) (Fall, 1988): 4–19.

Lacan, J. (1988). A materialist definition of the phenomenon of consciousness. In: J.-A. Miller (Ed.), S. Tomaselli (Trans.), *The Seminar of Jacques Lacan Book 2* (pp. 40–52). Cambridge: Cambridge University Press.

Langer, S. (1942). *Philosophy in a New Key.* Cambridge, MA: Harvard University Press.

Laplanche, J. (1997). The theory of seduction and the problem of the Other. *International Journal of Psychoanalysis, 78:* 653–666.

Laplanche, J., & Pontalis, J. B. (1973). *The Language of Psycho-analysis.* London: Hogarth.

Ogden, T. (1986). *The Matrix of the Mind: Object Relations and the Psychoanalytic Dialogue.* New York: Jason Aronson.

Renik, O. (1998). The analyst's subjectivity and the analyst's objectivity. *International Journal of Psychoanalysis, 79:* 487–497.

Segal, H. (1957). Notes on symbol formation. *International Journal of Psychoanalysis, 38:* 391–397.

Steiner, J. (1993). *Psychic Retreats.* London: Routledge.

Tronick, E. Z., & Weinberg, M. K. (1997). Depressed mothers and infants: failure to form dyadic states of consciousness. In: L. Murray & P. Cooper (Eds.), *Post-Partum Depression and Child Development.* New York: Guilford.

Winnicott, D. W (1945). Primitive emotional development. *International Journal of Psychoanalysis, 26*: 137–143.

Winnicott, D. W. (1953). Transitional objects and transitional phenomena—a study of the first not-me possession. *International Journal of Psychoanalysis, 34*: 89–97.

Wright, K. (1991). *Vision and Separation: Between Mother and Baby.* London: Free Association.

CHAPTER FIVE

A psychoanalytic approach to perception

Cesar Botella and Sara Botella

Editor's introduction

We have seen in the preceding chapters that, from the beginning of psychoanalysis, symbols were seen as representing something. This enables them to have a communicative function provided that what it is that they are taken to represent remains constant between the two minds communicating. In 2005, Cesar and Sara Botella published a book titled *The Work of Psychic Figurability*, which sought to offer new ways of thinking about mental states without representation. Figurability was a neologism created to cope with the difficulty in translating the German *darstellbarkeit*, which was one of the four mechanisms contributing to the "dream work" described by Freud (1900a) in *The Interpretation of Dreams*. The other three—condensation, displacement, and secondary revision—were retained in the English translation but it seems that Strachey's difficulty in translating *darstellbarkeit* meant that something was lost in translation.

The significance of the Botellas' book is that it enabled the identification of a process by which mental states in which there seemed to be no representation could be understood as communicable and in this sense open to interpretation and exploration. They place representation at the centre of their thoughts.

Thus: In "Negation" (1925h), Freud maintains the theoretical position he advanced in 1915 and adds that:

> The first and immediate aim, therefore, of reality testing is, not to *find* an object in real perception which corresponds to the one presented, but to refind such an object, to convince oneself that it is still there. [p. 237]

As long as the reality ego cannot confirm sufficiently that the object presented still exists, and also in reality, the perception remains persecuting for the pleasure ego. Moreover, the object's absence cannot be recognized and will be traumatic as long as the object presentation is maintained by the pleasure ego. *Indeed, in our view, it is not the loss of the object but the danger of its loss of representation and, by extension, the risk of non-representation, which denotes distress.*

The Botellas therefore place the capacity to represent at the heart of understanding mental health. It seems to me that this places an accent not just upon the intrapsychic significance of representation but also upon its interpsychic significance; that is, the possibility of communicating with another subject. The book describes working with autistic children and offers clinical material that illustrates how the psychoanalyst's work of figurability can be harnessed to gain access to states of mind in which there is memory without recollection. The book is a complex one, and it would be presumptuous to seek to summarize it here. However, there is a short chapter on the psychoanalytic view of perception that emphasizes the importance of keeping in mind that perception is an active process. It is this chapter that is reproduced here.

We have been looking in earlier chapters at some of the conceptual difficulties in separating objectivity and subjectivity. This chapter reminds us that we cannot, as Freud well knew, expect to be able to know the world—external or internal. Since the 1940s, it has been known that only a proportion of information reaching the eye actually is passed to the brain, which suggests that some kind of filter is exercised to prevent the brain being overwhelmed with information. However, we can expect to be able to learn about the internal and external worlds and, further, how we can come to know about them and what influences there are on what we know—or let ourselves know.

This chapter, being part of a complex book, should be taken as being presented here to emphasize that a symbol—or a representation, being uniquely a phenomenon of the subjective, demands something of the subject who perceives it. The corollary of this is that if communication is to be achieved, then work will be required first to create the symbol and then to perceive its meaning.

* * *

"The primary memory of a perception is always a hallucination"

(Freud, 1895, p. 339)

"Perception plays the part which in the id falls to instinct"

(Freud, 1923a, p. 25)

The unknowable

Whatever the means used to gain knowledge of the world, whether it be the sense organs or thinking, the problem is that knowledge has to fulfil certain conditions in order to lead to what Freud calls consciousness—that is to say, it has to acquire the characteristics of a form that is perceptible to consciousness. However psychical it may be, consciousness is none the less looked on by Freud as a "sense organ for the apprehension of psychical qualities" (Freud, 1900a, p. 574). The subject is far from being simple, for excitatory material "flows", he continues,

> into the Cs, sense organ from the *Pcpt.* system, whose excitation ... is probably submitted to a fresh revision before it becomes a conscious sensation, and from the interior of the apparatus itself, whose quantitative processes are felt qualitatively in the pleasure–unpleasure series when, subject to certain modifications, they make their way to consciousness. [*ibid.*, p. 616]

In both cases there is transformation of the initial product; the unknowable is generated at all levels:

In its innermost nature it is as much unknown to us as the reality
of the external world, and it is as incompletely presented by the
data of consciousness as is the external world by the communication of our senses organs. [*ibid.*, p. 613]

The human being can only know the object, whether internal or
external, from the emanations, the qualities emerging from the
sense organs, characteristics in a state of evolution that have repercussions on his consciousness; but these sensible and perceptible
qualities, which can be verbalized or represented visually, differ
from the object itself.

The unknowable is inevitably an integral part of the psyche. It
originates as much in the problem of perceptions closely dependent
on the sense organs and their limits as in that of the limits of
thought. At the outset, deprived of the quality of consciousness,
thought has to transform itself into preconscious thought in order
to acquire such a quality, which requires its passage via word-
presentations and their perceptual residues, especially auditory.
The drama of thought is that, in order to accede to the quality
consciousness, it is submitted to the double diktat of the sense
organs and the obligatory detour via perceptual qualities capable
of arousing consciousness. Between lure and transformation, the
unknowable is perpetuated. The "dream navel" bears witness to
this. The domain of what can be represented is a crude reduction of
the vast domain of the unknowable. The problem is thus no longer
one of the knowledge of an absolute and unattainable exterior.
Rather, what is at stake is knowledge at the level of the capacity of
the psychical apparatus and its degree of reliability for reflecting,
via the intermediary of representation and the quality consciousness, something of this unknowable domain. The study of thinking,
notably in its association with perception, has become a fundamental issue for both psychoanalysis and science.

Fifteen years after *The Interpretation of Dreams*, Freud (1915c)
suggested that psychoanalysts were, from the outset, in possession
of means that give them a certain advantage over scientists:

We shall be glad to learn that the correction of internal perception
will turn out not to offer such great difficulties as the correction of
external perception—that internal objects are less unknowable than
the external world. [Freud, 1915c, p. 171]

Owing to certain characteristics of their daily practice—the fact, for instance, that their object of study is the *Ucs.* of the "similar other", an external object that is, however, similar to the observer; and that their objectivity involves the observation of their own subjectivity and functioning during the observation—psychoanalysts find themselves at the centre of the contemporary scientific debates on knowledge. Due to their increasingly thorough understanding of how the psyche functions, they can—and perhaps should—rise to the challenge, in the near future, of making a considerable contribution to scientists. This they could do by providing better knowledge of the instrument and its limits so that the gap between what is perceived through observation and the object itself might be better identified. In other words, our approach to reality itself, to its "unknowable" nature, could be refined.

Bion was the first to take this path. In order to have access, however small, to the unknowable, in order to reach what lies beyond or short of sensory reality, of the representable, Kant's noumen or thing-in-itself, which Bion calls the "point O", the psyche, he suggests, has to operate not by means of the senses but through an "act of faith" on the part of the analyst, which he considers similar to that of mystical practice. We discussed in Part Three the great interest but also the dangers entailed in this comparison between mysticism and psychoanalysis. But whatever one may think of it, it cannot be denied that Bion managed to centre the problem of the knowledge of reality on the study of thinking; and to impose, as its corollary, the necessity of not circumscribing the latter to the dynamic of representations.

In parallel with the expansion of contemporary scientific thinking, which is obliged to try to transcend its own limits so that it can approach both the domain of the infinitely small as well as that of the infinitely great, psychoanalysts have understood during recent years that the limits of their means of thinking and those of their knowledge converge and are inseparable. Hence their effort to take interest in how their own psyche functions in the analytic situation, in the hope of finding a means of gaining access to the comprehension of a psychical dimension and sufferings other than those of neurosis—a domain where intelligibility refers neither to certain expected causalities nor to the notion of representation alone.

The irrepresentable

It may seem paradoxical that psychoanalysts write about the irrepresentable, so much is analytic theory determined by the notion of representation and, in particular, by the sense it has of unconscious representation. A certain number of questions arise immediately: what is the relation between the metapsychological concept of unconscious representation and this notion of irrepresentability that has appeared so often in the analytic writings of recent years? In an analytic theory that claims to be rigorous, should one not envisage that the irrepresentable is nothing other than one of the characteristics of unconscious representation; and, in this case, is not all this interest in the irrepresentable exaggerated or unjustified? Or, alternatively, this appreciation is summary and, beyond the fascination that such a suggestive term, with its romantic aura, can exert, the preoccupation of analytic authors for the irrepresentable is the consequence of an increasingly fine analysis of the metapsychology of the session and a fresh awareness of the role in the treatment of the limits of the psychical apparatus and its capacities for representation. However that may be, what can be said here and now is that the irrepresentable can seemingly be defined only in terms of a singular negativity of representation that includes the latter; and, consequently, the study of irrepresentability rightly falls to psychoanalysts and refers them to the indispensable prior condition of establishing a definition of representation from a specifically analytic point of view.

The real problem begins here, for throughout Freud's entire work, the notion of representation remained rather imprecise and was impregnated with diverse meanings. He used the term as it is habitually used. The notion of representation sometimes has the sense, in his writings, of the psychical repetition of an external perception and sometimes the more sophisticated sense of delegation (the psychical representative of the drive). It is this last sense, only, which would be given a definition of a strictly metapsychological order: the concept of *Vorstellungsrepräsentant* was to be indissociable from primal repression and would determine what constitutes the system *Ucs.* itself. It is thus in this respect that analytic theory, for better or worse, one might say, is closely and inextricably bound up with the notion of representation. Without going any further, we could then conclude that, in analytic writings, the use of the term irrepresentable should be reserved for that which does not fall within the scope of this *Vorstellungsrepräsentant*, for that which has no possibility of gaining access to a chain of representations governed by unconscious wishes, by the drive and its fixation to its psychical representative.

Defining itself by the foundational concept of "unconscious representation", analytic theory is organized around a paradox: it seeks to maintain, within the same concept, both the idea of a representation located in the unconscious and, by definition, cut off from consciousness, and the opposite idea, contained in the term representation, of "presenting before the eyes or before the mind". It is this semantic irreconcilability that radically differentiates analytic theory from any other discipline. Dialogue with other sciences will thus pose apparently insurmountable problems, not so much due, as it has often been thought, to resistance in scientists towards psychoanalysis, originating in their own repressions, but due to this conception that is deeply incompatible with the rationality necessary for all positivist scientific thought, at least in the form it has taken up to a short time ago. Perhaps now, with the revolution introduced by relativity, quantum theory, and their repercussions profoundly modifying scientific thinking, dialogue has become possible between analysts and scientists. We like to imagine that analytic theory, with its major concept of unconscious representation, can be the first model, at the heart of the evolution of scientific thought, of a new conception of science that is capable of breaking with the limits imposed by preconscious logic, temporo-spatiality, and the ego's need for tangible evidence.

Caught then, as it is, between one definition, that of the delegation of an *Ucs.*, by definition unknown and inaccessible in itself, and another, that of the reproduction of an external world, the study of representation, and, consequently, of the irrepresentable, psychoanalytic theory is faced with considerable problems: those of knowledge, consciousness, and perception, all notions that have been given little treatment in psychoanalytic literature.

In 1938, in line with the spirit of science that was already modern, Freud asserted that:

In the meantime we try to increase the efficiency of our sense organs to the furthest possible extent by artificial aids; but it may be expected that all such efforts will fail to effect the ultimate outcome. Reality will always remain "unknowable". [1940a (1938), p. 196]

This observation is still valid today, in spite of the spectacular progress of science, as Bernard d'Espagnat (1990, 1994) concludes. The same can also be said of all those in other domains who endeavour to approach reality. The description made by the Nobel Prize-winning novelist, Camilo José Cela (1990), is exemplary:

But things are never described as they are, but only as they are perceived. The essence of a bit of grass, for instance, remains a mystery for man, an inaccessible Arcanum. And yet we define it and reduce it to its green colour, its form, its flexibility or its bitter taste. [Interview in *Le Figaro*, 27 August]

And so we are faced, not without a certain sense of perplexity, with the problem of a reality that is "unknowable", while at the same time being the source of our perceptions. What is more, this source of perceptions is charged with a sense of self-evidence, of certitude as to the existence of the lost object, of unshakeable truth. In other words, however "unknowable" reality is for man, it none the less brings him a certain type of knowledge from which he can no longer free himself. It could be said that, just as the falcon lured by the bait returns to the hand, the psyche is trained by the lure of the sense organs.

The scientist has recourse to particular languages, like mathematics, in order to be able to conceptualize certain external elements that are independent of the sense organs, whether they are the universe or the infinitely small. Indeed, every man uses word-presentations, whether absolute or infinite, that have a meaning for him, although he is incapable of imagining their content. In parallel to this, in so far as his internal world is concerned, he is faced with experience that he cannot easily represent, and poetry or music will be the means of approaching them. It is a matter, in all cases, of the limits of our systems of representation. But this is only of relative interest to psychoanalysts, for the specificity of analytic research resides, above all, in the study of the *Ucs.* and, in a more general way, in the study of psychical inscriptions more than in the study of their means of expression.

We know that studying the mechanisms of neurosis leads us to the comprehension of our psychic functioning in relation to the instances and causalities between the representative contents that are part of the neurotic structure. In this context, the term irrepresentable defines a content with a meaning that can eventually be named but not represented—words like absolute or infinite would be the model for this. But analytic practice teaches us that when listening to the whole range of the experience of the session, without limiting this to the comprehension of the underlying relations of the neurosis, the irrepresentable becomes something different, that is, neither content nor meaning. The very term irrepresentable turns out to be improper from this perspective. In fact, in this wider context of the session, what we understand by irrepresentable can be signified only in terms of a negativity.

In *Inhibitions, Symptoms and Anxiety* (1925a, p. 170) Freud writes, "Thus, the first determinant of anxiety, which the ego itself introduces, is loss of the perception of the object (which is equated with loss of the object itself)". Following this model, and extending Freud's conception, we wrote at the beginning of this book that the loss of the perception of the object cannot be traumatic as long as its representation is maintained; that it is not the loss of the perception of the object but the loss of its representation, the danger of *non-representation*, that is the mark of infantile distress.

We can see, then, how the problem of knowledge, that is, of knowing what the relations are between the observer and the observed, between the inside and the outside, boils down to an investigation of the laws that organize the relations between perception and representation. The problem of knowledge necessarily entails the study of perception, which is inseparable from the study of consciousness.

This being the case, the original question concerning psychoanalysts and their way of envisaging irrepresentability now returns in another form: is the notion irrepresentable simply the sign of a sense of impotence in relation to our current knowledge and, in this case, can the irrepresentable be surpassed each time that our knowledge progresses? Or, on the contrary, is it irrevocably the ultimate representation possible of our psychical reality, marking the limits of what can be represented, and of thinking at its most abstract?

A brief reminder on perception

Throughout Freud's work, perception as well as its definition suffer, as we know, from a certain lack of rigour. In this, his work merely reflects a problem of a general nature: that none of the different definitions of perception is entirely satisfying. Accordingly, it is sometimes envisaged as the very act of the sense organs and sometimes as content. The latter can thus be considered in psychoanalysis as a signifying content referring to an infantile sexual theory and to a basic complex of infantile psychoneurosis. Is it because of this diversification, this indetermination, that, after Freud, psychoanalysts were not tempted to study perception? At any rate, the real difficulty is probably due to the specific nature of our psychoanalytic discipline, which is essentially constructed as a theory of representation and, further, of unconscious representation; that is to say, of repressed phantasy charged with prohibited instinctual impulses. It is a theoretical corpus whose formulations are particularly far removed from any psychological notion, such as perception.

However, at certain moments in the development of his theory, Freud was himself obliged to introduce the problem of perception. Apart from the 'Project for a scientific psychology' (1895), a pre-analytic text, and *The Interpretation of Dreams* (1900a), which inaugurated psychoanalytic theory, it was above all during the 1914–1918 war, when he was confronted with the study of traumatic neurosis and with the hallucinatory repetition in dreams of a traumatic perception. Then, during the 1920s, Freud set about the difficult task of establishing a meta-psychology of the distinction inside–outside, through the study of psychosis initially, followed shortly after by the study of fetishism and the disavowal of perception involved. This shows *a posteriori* that psychosis and perversion were of less interest to Freud in themselves than as means of broaching the relations of the psyche with the real world. (For more details on the relation of Freudian theory to perception, see Green, 1999, pp. 202, 211.)

Today, psychoanalysts are at last concerning themselves with the problem of perception, led not, as one might suppose, by the expansion of cognitivism, but by a movement specific to their own preoccupations which has its roots in Freud's reflections on traumatic neurosis and the disavowal of perception. In fact, far from being the initiator, the expansion of cognitivism may be said, rather, to have had an inhibiting role for psychoanalysts. For perception involves a risk of deviating towards a new model of the treatment where observation of the concrete, of products arising solely from a relation based on the concreteness of the sense organs—like the psychoanalyst who, in good faith, observes attentively the facial expression of his analysand in order to discover an affect, a hidden meaning—would take precedence over the free-floating attention allowing the analyst to listen to the analysand's unconscious phantasy and, in a more general way, to the changes of levels in the different modes of representation (*représentance*) of the psychoanalyst's thinking. In short, such a research model would sweep aside the determining and organizing components of the analytic process that are inaccessible to any form of direct observation, however fine it may be. In this respect Winnicott's practice is exemplary. Even though he was always very fond of baby observation and extremely attentive to the play activities of children, he always maintained that it was the transference, exclusively, that held the key to the understanding of the psyche. It is not by observing the sleeper, even by means of the most sophisticated recording techniques, that the dream becomes visible, even less its meaning.

There is a risk of going adrift each time one neglects the fact that psychoanalysis is the fruit of a very particular evolution in the practice of Freud, who was distancing himself increasingly from medicine and phenomenology. A series of renunciations concerning perception gave rise to psychoanalysis—the medical exam, hypnosis, suggestion, pressures applied to the forehead were all abandoned—and then, Freud's stroke of genius in withdrawing out of the patient's view, the analytic setting comes into being and is maintained on the condition that it is determined by not being able to see the analyst, by the fact that the perceptions of the sense organs are reduced to a minimum, so as to facilitate the emergence of internal psychic life, the dimension of representation and phantasy. This places psychoanalysis in a specific and thoroughly original position for studying perception.

In reality, there is, surprisingly, much less distance today between psychoanalysis and certain trends of cognitivism and neurobiology than there used to be. Especially when one thinks of the 1970s, and the temptation at that time, particularly in the USA, with Hubert Dreyfus, of translating psychoanalysis into cognitivist terms. By establishing an oversimplified connection, to say the least, between psychoanalysis and cognitivism, the Freudian notion of representation was reduced and confused with that of Brentano, on the pretext that Freud had attended his courses in Vienna. And Dreyfus went so far as to associate the tendency towards fulfilment, specific to the representations located in the system *Ucs.*, with the idea of intentionality, an idea which, as we know, also came from Brentano and constituted thereafter the basis of the thinking of another pupil of the same epoch, Husserl. To come to the conclusion, on the basis of these facts, that, in its very conception, psychoanalysis is cognitivist, proves the readiness of some to ignore the Freudian theory of the unconscious, whether it is the *Ucs.* as a system of the first topography, or, as from 1923 (*The Ego and the Id*), the *Ucs.* integrated within a much larger whole, the id, a new psychical agency in which drive activity is then described without being linked to representational systems. And even if one takes into account the fact that "an instinct can never become an object of consciousness—only the idea that represents the instinct can" (1915e, p. 177)—one cannot forget the role of affect, which can also be a representative of the drive. Things become more complex if, following Green (1986), one accepts that: "the object reveals the drive". Far from being a mere reproduction of a perception, and notwithstanding certain passages in Freud that tend in this direction, Freudian representation is considered today by the majority of authors as a vast network of meaning constituted, under the influence of infantile sexuality, through transformation of the represented instinctual acitivity of the id. The recent reduction operated by Erdelyi (1985), cited by Varela (1988), applying cognitivist terminology to the Freudian concept of repression, is yet another outrageous simplification. As for the ideas of Davidson and Dennett and the notion of a "mind without a subject", we refer the reader to the excellent critique offered by André Green in his article "Philosophie de l'esprit et psychanalyse" (1996).

Fortunately, an important current of theoreticians from the cognitive sciences has become increasingly aware that, however neurobiological and rooted in so-called objective information perception may be, its theorization cannot for all that escape the conditions of the very particular relations established between what is perceived and the perceiver and between what is perceived and knowledge. In this sense, the majority of scientists today accept that, while perception certainly depends on sensory receptors, it cannot be confined to them. Local physiological responses are far from being capable alone of defining the complexity of the perceptual process that, including the psychical, has to be understood at a global level. Psychoanalysts are not the only ones to assert this; recent works of neurobiologists, those of Ecclés and Edelman, as well as those of Francis Crick, come to similar conclusions. Indeed, at the present time, most authors agree in considering that perception cannot be conceived as a simple entry of information in the central nervous system: "it is the brain and not the environment which decides what we see" (Barlow, 1990, cited by Bourguignon, 1994). Jeannerod (1993) was more precise:

> It is not the environment which solicits the nervous system, shapes it or reveals it. On the contrary, it is the subject and his brain which question the environment, inhabit it gradually, and finally master it.

The same is true of the cognitive sciences: J.-P. Dupuy (1994) points out that, in 1948, McCulloch had already discovered that the eye only transmits to the brain a fraction of the information it receives; that the organism has to "pay in information" for gaining access to the certainty that there is a world that exists outside us. According to McCulloch, this loss is in fact programmed; and, according to Pitts, what we are dealing with here is a law of nature the existence of which translates its very great redundancy (McCulloch, 1948–1953). What is more, a tendency that is currently making its weight felt within the cognitive sciences proposes a functional approach that even goes as far as formulating the hypothesis that perceptual processes are characterized by psychical "constructions". Thus, Francisco Varela (1988) asserts that: "Perceiving is the equivalent of constructing invariants by a sensory–motor coupling which permits the organism to survive in its environment". And, in 1994, this same author concluded that the basis of cognition is an autonomous "global activity":

> It is this autonomous activity of the system that needs to be put at the centre of our investigations, rather than our entries . . . The key

point consists in considering as central, and not as a secondary problem, the question of the interpretation, the emergence of meaning . . . It is no longer a question of the information which is given, but of the information as something which is literally in-formed (formed from within); and it is this creation of meaning as an autonomous activity which is capable of accounting for what is most interesting in knowledge.

One cannot be more explicit and the psychoanalyst can only be delighted by this perspective, for it corresponds to a path that psychoanalysis has explored since its creation: hallucination. An explanation is necessary here. Owing to the fact that dream hallucination excludes perception, there is a tendency to oppose perception and hallucination or to reduce hallucination to an error of judgement concerning perception. However, it is being understood increasingly that the relations between them are far from simple. Thus very recently, Jeannerod, who directs the Inserm (Institut national de la santé et de la recherche médicale) research unit "Vision et Motility", declared in an interview for the journal *La Recherche* (Jeannerod, 1996) that, by using techniques of cerebral imagery applied to patients who were hallucinating, he had been able to discover that

hallucinations activate the primary zones of perception, the very ones which process external sensory information . . . whereas one might have imagined that hallucinations activate neither the receptive zones, nor the executive zones, but rather the central regions managing "second hand" information . . . This means that perceiving an object and imagining it is in the end the same thing.

This astonishing relation between perception and hallucination has not escaped René Angelergues (1992), who asserts that "Perception is hallucination". René Diatkine taught us a long time ago, in the form of jest, that perception is a perversion of hallucination. In the same vein, we have been interested in the idea defended by John Steward (1994) that, "the capacities of cognition are ultimately hallucinatory". The same idea may be found in one of the conclusions established by Isabelle Billiard (1994), concerning the meetings of a multi-disciplinary workgroup in which she urges psychoanalysts to "reconsider from a different point of view the question of the primal mode of being of psychical activity, that is, its hallucinatory capacity". This is of special interest to us because, through purely psychoanalytic means of reflection and through the experience of treatments of neurotics and borderline cases, this idea was one we also defended during a UNESCO Conference in 1989. We insisted then on the need for analytic theory to introduce the notion of the hallucinatory as a process beyond or short of the representational and the perceptual, of which it is both a source and a result. Nothing in the psyche would take place without the participation of the hallucinatory, including perceptual processes.

The relation perception-consciousness

Although there is undeniably a general tendency in psychoanalysis, even in Freud, to reduce perception to an elementary function, to a non-complex unity, the notion is at the same time used in other senses: self-perception, endopsychic perception, internal perception, or, again, perception specific to the id.

As for the notion of consciousness, it is defined in *The Interpretation of Dreams*, as we have already recalled, as a "sense-organ for the perception of psychical qualities" (Freud, 1900a, p. 615). As an organ, it remains, throughout almost the whole of Freud's work, united with perception, constituting one and the same system, the *Pcs.–Cs*, situated at the periphery of the psychical apparatus of which "consciousness is the subjective side of one part of the physical processes in the nervous system, namely of the perceptual processes" (1895, p. 311). Then, once he was involved in the study of the unconscious, Freud no longer really interested himself in either of them and they were practically left on one side until 1915. Then, in the space of ten days (according to the *Standard Edition* between 23 April and 4 May exactly), Freud simultaneously wrote "Mourning and melancholia" (1917b) and "A metapsychological supplement to the theory of dreams: (1917a) (and they were published in the same edition of the *Internationale Zeitschrift Psychoanalysus*). These were two fundamental texts and their confrontation opened the way towards a new theoretical conception. In the latter, the union of perception and consciousness is asserted, but an inversion occurs in what Freud now calls the system consciousness–perception (*Bewusstsein–Wahrnehmung*), giving priority to *Cs.* over psychical processes. This was probably the consequence of a new objective that Freud had given himself by writing the "Metapsychological supplement". Instead of focusing his interest on the dream content and its interpretation, as he had done until then, and being concerned to acquaint himself increasingly with the functioning of repression and that of the system *Ucs.*, he now gave priority to the processual, to the study of the hallucinatory quality of dreams, by linking the latter up with the theory of narcissism elaborated one year earlier. Dream hallucination was thus no longer understood solely as a product of formal or topographical regression; it acquired the status of a narcissistic process.[1]

We get a measure of the complexity of the Freudian approach—which never falls into the temptation of simplification and often treats the subject at a certain level of explicit elaboration while, at the same time, remaining open implicitly to other solutions—if we take into account the fact that, during these same ten days, in "Mourning and melancholia", which truly complements the "Metapsychological supplement", Freud tried to situate the notion of the object at the centre of analytic theory; that is, he opened the latter to the link with the external world. Thus, with these two articles which close his papers on metapsychology, initiating a notion of perception closely bound up with narcissism, hallucinatory in nature, and open to the world, a psychoanalytic approach to traumatic neurosis became possible and the premises of the second topography were laid.

After an extension in *Beyond the Pleasure Principle* (1920g), where one again comes across the priority of the system *Cs.*, it was in *The Ego and the Id* (1923b) that perception took precedence definitively. There it is either a question solely of the system *Pcs.* or of an inversion of the formula used in the "Metapsychological supplement: of the system *Pcpt.–Cs. (Wahrnehmung–Bewusstsein)*. The articles that follow, i.e., those devoted to the loss of reality in neuroses and psychoses or the article on the "mystic writing-pad", or again "Negation" (1925b), bear witness to Freud's growing interest in perception. This evolution was confirmed and concluded in *New Introductory Lectures on Psychoanalysis* (1933a), in which Freud, studying this subject for the last time, openly grants perception its autonomy, the right to be a system in itself, the system *Pcpt.* (*Wahrnehmung*) and maintains, as he does in the "Project", that "during its functioning the phenomenon of consciousness arises in it" (1933a, p. 75); that is to say, consciousness becomes a quality of the system *Pcs.* The schema at the end of the chapter is evidence of this; it reproduces the schema in *The Ego and the Id* (1923b), although consciousness does not appear in it.

But it was his investigations into the perversion of fetishism (1927e) that would offer him the possibility of really approaching the connection between the ego and reality and of coming to terms with the complexity of the role of perception. By constituting a fetishistic object, the fetishist acknowledges in his own way the missing penis in a woman and thus accords sense perception its full importance; but, at the same time, he retains, in his endopsychic perception, something irrepresentable and terrifying from his infantile sexuality, the anti-traumatic outcome of which is the belief that women do have a penis. Gilbert Diatkine (1994) has already pointed out that Freud's conception of perception then undergoes a change. In fact, due to this possible division between sense perception and endopsychic perception, the study of perception can no longer be reduced to one of a sensory content in as much as the endopsychic perception can simultaneously have a different content.

The ambiguity of the notion of consciousness considered both as a system and as a quality was thus removed; henceforth consciousness could be conceived of as that which, during the functioning of the system *Pcs.*, detaches itself from it and, momentarily, becomes quality.

An important question persists, none the less: how are we to define perception as a system, to describe its dynamics and, in particular, its relations with consciousness, when perception and consciousness do not lend themselves at all easily to temporo–spatial metaphors, to being part of a schema, their main characteristics being immediateness, atemporality, the absence of permanent investment? Just as, for the spectator, "the dancer and the dance are one", perception and consciousness cannot establish a distinction between what is perceived and the process under way. The problem is one of knowing whether the metapsychological apparatus, as Freud handed it down to us, is really able to take this into account.

Freud was certainly not taken in by this problem or by the manner in which he was obliged—courageously, considering the scientific thinking of his time and the rigorous character he wanted to give to the metapsychology—to leave certain concepts somewhat vague, with a possibility of contradiction, if he wanted to pass on to us the most exact approach to the functioning of the psyche. Indeed, the true coherence of the metapsychology and, more broadly, of Freud's thought, resides as much in its rigorous character as in its capacity to integrate a tolerance for openness to new possibilities and developments. This is undeniably the case for the evolution concerning the character of perception and consciousness.

As we know, consciousness, like the sense organs, is only excitable under certain conditions; without their presence, it is incapable of perceiving psychical activity; it does not even have the slightest suspicion as to its existence. These conditions that are capable of awakening the quality consciousness depend on a phenomenon whose essential aspect is the investment of attention, the link with presentations, those of words principally; and more exactly to "memories of words", says Freud, thereby linking the problem of the quality consciousness with the system of memory, in short, with the inevitable temporo–spatiality without which the phenomenon of consciousness cannot occur. Thus the exacerbation of the investment of attention maintains a strong link with the quality consciousness. But that is not all: what is important, says Freud, in the *Outline* is that:

> [S]ince memory-traces can become conscious just as perceptions do, especially through their association with residues of speech, the possibility arises of a confusion which would lead to a mistaking of reality. The ego guards itself against this possibility by the institution of *reality-testing* . . . [Freud, 1940a, p. 199]

The distinction representation–perception is a permanent and arduous task of the ego and all the more essential in that it is erased periodically during regressive states in sleep when, as is made clear in "Metapsychological supplement to the theory of dreams", as the system *Cs.* is uncathected and reality testing is abandoned, "the excitations which, independently of the state of sleep, have entered on the path of regression, will find that path clear as far as the system *Cs.* where they will count as undisputed reality" (1917d, p. 234).

And Freud himself immediately acknowledges in a footnote the theoretical impasse implied by this observation:

> Here the principle of the insusceptibility of excitation of uncathected systems appears to be invalidated in the case of the system *Cs. (Pcpt.)*. But it may be a question of only the *partial* removal of cathexis; and for the perceptual system in especial we must assume many conditions of excitation which are widely divergent from those of other systems. [*ibid.*]

There exist, then, two ways of achieving endoperception: either in the waking state, via residues, the sensory residues of words and things, or in the retrogressive state when excitations are subjected to another treatment.

The retrogressive psychic state, momentarily cut off from these cathexes, represents a certain perceptual quality that can also manifest itself in daytime, notably in the regressive conditions of the session. With a "partial withdrawal of cathexis from the system *Cs.*", accompanied by a "partial" abandonment of reality testing, a quite original quality can occur during the day—that is, a capacity for intelligibility, which, without the participation of primary and secondary processes, beyond sensory experience, without having right of access, along the forward, progressive path, to the quality of representation and to the system *Pcs.-Cs.*, offers a direct path of access to endopsychic perception, to the accessibility of certain mental "zones" that are otherwise unreachable.

In the 1980s, with the study of border concepts (*concepts-limites*) such as negative hallucination (Green, 1983), the perception of the lack (Braunschweig & Fain, 1975; Fain, 1982), the zero imago and apophatism (Pasche, 1983), or again, our own concept of *nonrepresentation* (Botella & Botella, 1983), there appeared in French analytic literature what might be described as a relativization of the stability of the topographies and of their dependence both on the direction and the scale of time and on the hegemony of the content; for all these concepts have emerged from research into the erasure or collapse of the systems of representations.[2]

The usefulness of privileging the study of these border concepts becomes all the clearer now that we know, since our study of *non-representation*, that the absence of representable content does not mean an absence of an event. What was suggested by the evolution of Freud's thought now becomes clear. In order to study perception and consciousness, as well as the deep connections between perception and representation, we can no longer continue to limit our thinking to the classic conception of the psychical apparatus and to the specific points of view of the metapsychology.

From perception to the perceptual process

We were saying earlier just how imprecise the notion of perception remained in Freud's work. It inevitably stands in a difficult relationship with analytic theory owing to the fact that the latter is centred on representation, leaving it only a marginal place. Located at the limits of our theory, disliked by psychoanalysts, entirely ignored by the index of the *Abstracts of the Standard Edition*, only figuring in *The Language of Psychoanalysis* by Laplanche and Pontalis under the heading of "consciousness" (psychological), and considered by many as a notion that should be left to psychologists, neurophysiologists, or cognitivists, it has never been the object of a truly psychoanalytic study.

In terms of content, its status is relatively clear: a traumatic content or a primal content necessary to the organization of the psyche. Freud's insistence on the role of perception for the constitution of the principal phantasies, castration and the primal scene—for one, the sight of the difference between the sexes; for the other, certain evocative signs—bears witness to the importance that he accorded to it. The two phases of the complex of castration comprise not only a gap in time and consequently a work of memory, and thus of elaboration, but also the participation of the simultaneous perception of the present and the past. In order for phantasy to organize itself at the heart of the infantile neurosis on which it is founded, it is indispensable to be able to recall seeing the difference between the sexes at the moment of hearing the threat that had hitherto been inoperative; or conversely, to recall hearing the threat of castration on seeing the difference between the sexes that until then had remained indifferent. And if the reality of perception does not appear in ontogenesis, phylogenesis will take charge of it.

Let us return, however, to one of the major problems, already raised, that Freud handed down to us: how are we to conceive of perception as a system, that is, as an integral part of the psychical apparatus like the other systems, preconscious and unconscious, when the term system presupposes the idea of a "set of elements which depend reciprocally on each other in such a way as to form an organised whole" (Lalande) that does not correspond to the nature of the relations of perception? Instead, Green (1993) proposes that:

> [T]he perceptual quality be considered from the angle of "making present to oneself" which infers . . . implying a change of state and a plurality of modes of existence, each of which can take over from the other, without linking these to a "conscious" phenomenon. We shall thus be freed from this aspect of immediateness which perceptual experience comes up against in contrast to the discursiveness of understanding. Perception is discursive, just as thought needs to become perceptible to be thought about. [pp. 212–213]

In order to cover this vast field of the perceptual quality, we will make use of a more general term, that of the perceptual, which we will employ in the sense of *The Interpretation of Dreams* (1900a, p. 499), based on a citation already used, but whose importance obliges us to repeat it:

> Our waking (preconscious) thinking behaves towards any perceptual material with which it meets in just the same way in which the function we are considering behaves towards the content of dreams [i.e. secondary revision]. It is the nature of our waking thought to establish order in material of that kind, to set up relations in it and to make it conform to our expectations of an intelligible whole.

This, then, is how Freud freed himself right away from the limits of a psychological conception and opened up the metapsychology of perception to a conception akin to that of dreams, to be more exact, of the dream-work, to what might be called the *"work of the perceptual"*. We subscribe to this, while none the less preferring to use, instead of work, the notion of *process*. By this we mean a set of phenomena presenting a certain unity, while taking account of the fact that perceptual processes depend on a psychic reality that includes as much the perception of the sense organs as endopsychic perception.[3]

The new understanding furnished by the study of fetishism, that is, the possibility of psychic functioning operating through the simultaneity of two perceptual processes, with different meaning and content, would at last enable Freud to analyse, in 1936, his disturbance of memory on the Acropolis that had occurred in 1904, more than thirty years earlier. It is one of the major texts of the Freudian corpus in which all the complexity of a multi-dimensional psychic universe could not be revealed in the brilliant analysis that Freud carried out so meticulously, highlighting the relationship, in simultaneity, between (a) memory, the endoperception of a recollection, "So all this really *does* exist, just as we learnt at school!"; (b) the barely stifled disavowal of the perception of the sense organs, "What I see here is not real"; and (c) "feelings of derealization" which he calls "complicated processes" and which are equivalent to phenomena of a hallucinatory order. At the end of this analysis of this disturbance of memory, protecting him from a split, an alteration of the self-presentation, Freud discovered just how intense the investment of an object-representation, the loved father, could be, and became aware of the sense of guilt involved in surpassing him. An immoderate infantile wish was at the origin of the onset of the disturbance, of the simultaneity of these different hallucinatory–perceptual processes, memory, disavowal, sensations of derealization, and the cause of the rupture of the equilibrium of what we will call, in the next chapter, the *symmetry representation–perception*—a situation akin to the case of the analysand we reported earlier under the title "the smell of fir".

Notes

1.   Perhaps this was also a way of reconsidering a crucial problem in connection with perception and already announced in the Project— namely, the conceptualization of the transformation of the quantitative into the qualitative. On the side of perception "the structure of the nervous system consists of contrivances for transforming external quantity into quality"; on the side of consciousness that "gives us what are called qualities", the same question arises: "How and where do

qualities originate?" This was a question that would never really be answered.

2. It is here that one will be able to measure the importance of Green's works on the metapsychology of limits and on the work of the negative. To facilitate their comprehension, we recommend reading J. E. Jackson's book, *De l'affect a la pensée. Introduction à l'oeuvre d'André Green*, Mercure de France, 1991

3. Likewise in *Totem and Taboo* (1912–1913, p. 95): "There is an intellectual function in us which demands unity, connection or intelligibility from any material, whether of perception or thought, that comes within its grasp; and if, as a result of special circumstances, it is unable to establish a true connection, it does hesitate to fabricate a false one."

References

Angelergues, R. (1992). *De l'hallucination au langage*. Monograph No. 2 of the Evelyn and John Kestenberg Centre for Psychoanalysis.

Billiard, I. (1994). *Somatisations, psychanalyse et sciences de vivant*. Paris: Eshel.

Botella, C., & Botella, S. (1983). *Notes cliniques sur l'invertissement de la representation du mot*. Les Cahiers du Centre de Psychanalyse et de Psychtherapie.

Bourguignon, A. (1994). *L'homme imprévu, l'homme fou (histoire naturelle de l'homme)* Vols 1 & 2. Paris: Presses Universitaire de France.

Braunschweig, D., & Fain, M. (1975). *Le nuit, le jour*. Paris: Presses Universitaire de France.

Cela, C. J. (1990). Interview. *Le Figaro*, 27 August.

d'Espagnat, B. (1990). *Penser la science ou les enjeux de savoir*. Paris: Dunod.

d'Espagnat, B. (1994). *Le réel voilé*. Paris: Fayard.

Diatkine, G. (1994). *L'enfant dans l'adulte ou l'eternéel capacité de reverie*. Lonat: Delachaux et Niestle.

Dupuy, J. -P. (1994). *Aux origines des sciences cognitives*. Paris: La découverte.

Erdelyi, M. H. (1985). *Psychoanalysis: Freud's Cognitive Psychology*. New York: W. H. Freeman.

Fain, M. (1982). *Le désir de l'interprete*. Paris: Aubier-Montaigne.

Freud, S. (1895). A project for a scientific psychology. *S.E.*, 1: 283–397. London, Hogarth.

Freud, S. (1900a). *The Interpretation of Dreams*. *S.E.*, 4-5. London: Hogarth.

Freud, S. (1915c). Instincts and their vicissitudes. *S.E.*, *14*: 111–140. London: Hogarth.

Freud, S. (1915e). The unconscious. *S.E.*, *14*: 161–204. London: Hogarth.

Freud, S. (1917d). Metapsychological supplement to the theory of dreams. *S.E.*, *14*: 222–236. London: Hogarth.

Freud, S. (1920g). *Beyond the Pleasure Principle*. *S.E.*, *18*: 7–64. London: Hogarth.

Freud, S. (1923a). Two encylopaedia articles. *S.E.*, *18*: 233–259. London: Hogarth.

Freud, S. (1923b). *The Ego and the Id*. *S.E.*, *19*: 3–66. London: Hogarth.

Freud, S. (1925a). *Inhibitions, Symptoms and Anxiety*. *S.E.*, *20*. London: Hogarth.

Freud, S. (1927e). Fetishism. *S.E.*, *21*: 149–158. London: Hogarth.

Freud, S. (1933a). *New Introductory Lectures on Psychoanalysis*. *S.E.*, *22*. London: Hogarth.

Freud, S. (1938b). Some elementary lessons in psycho-analysis. *S.E.*, *23*: 281–286. London: Hogarth.

Freud, S. (1940a [1938]). *An Outline of Psycho-Analysis*. *S.E.*, *23*: 141–208. London: Hogarth.

Green, A. (1983). Pulsion de mort, narcissisme negatif, fonction des-objectalisanté. In: *La pulsion de mort*. Paris: Presses Universitaire de France.

Green, A. (1986). The dead mother. In: *On Private Madness*. London: Hogarth.

Greeen, A. (1996). Philosophie de l'esprit et psychanalyse. In: *Psychanalyse, neurosciences et cognitivismes*. Paris: Presses Universitaire de France.

Jeannerod, M. (1993). *Le cerveau machine: physiologie de la volonté*. Paris: Fayard.

Jeannerod, M. (1996). Un tremplin pour les sciences cognitives. De l'étude du relief cränien à l'analyse des fluctuations de débit sanguin. *La Recherche*, *289*: 22–25.

McCulloch, W. S. (1948–1953). Tenth Macy Conference on Cybernetics. H. von Foerster (ed.).

Steward, J. (1994). *Somatisations, psychanalyse et sciences de vivant*. Paris: Eshel.

Varela, F. (1988). *Connaître les sciences cognitives*. Paris: Seuil.

Varela, F. (1994). Sciences cognitives et psychanalyse: questions ouvertes. In: *Somatisations, psychanalyse et sciences de vivant*. Paris: Eshel.

CHAPTER SIX

A clinical paradox of absence in the transference: how some patients create a virtual object to communicate an experience

James Rose

Introduction: a clinical paradox

I t is comparatively common that someone will come to an initial therapeutic consultation describing themselves as depressed; suffering from a lack of confidence and feeling devoid of ambition. There seems to be nothing inside them. Their psychic life can appear to be pervaded with an anomie to the point that it seems surprising to the assessor that they have bothered to come to the consultation at all. Often there is evidence of disrupted family history, early bereavements, and separations. Despite the seemingly traumatic nature of these losses, these are often dismissed as unimportant because they happened "so long ago". In short, the assessor can see many reasons for their depressed state of mind, but there is an apparent gulf between that person's and the assessor's understanding that seems unbridgeable. It can leave the assessor feeling hopeless and impotent, feeling that he has nothing to give or contribute. There is, thus, an apparent emptiness in the counter-transference, which can seem the result of a deficit of functioning in the subject and it can appear that this person will not be able to use treatment because of their incapacity to symbolize or to reflect upon their experience, i.e., that there is something missing in them.

Paradoxically, these unpromising prospects often prove wrong, despite the initial rejection of interpretations of early loss. But, while the patient concerned becomes eventually engaged with a treatment process, change does not occur at a sparkling rate. Progress can be so slow that it appears non-existent, and the apparently stuck quality of their lives becomes replicated in the transference. These patients can appear to be saying "you can't help me", and yet they come for help—*and keep coming*.

One interpretation of this pattern might be that the patient wishes to evacuate a feeling of despair into the analyst. But the problem with this hypothesis is that, however it might be temporarily true, it does not stand the test of time because the pattern is continually repeated for no apparent reason or gain to the patient or external compulsion. The question, then, is how to conceptualize theoretically a paradoxical pattern in which a patient persists in coming to tell their analyst that they cannot help them. Is it possible that a patient's psychic life can be determined by something that is absent as much as something that is present? If so, how does this occur?

To communicate this absence to the psychoanalyst, the patient seems to have to be in some sense absent. Alternatively, we might think that the patient who persists in saying "you can't help me" could be in some way perverse or destructive—but then how do we understand not only their real sense of frustration, but also the fact that they come for help at all, when there is no compulsion to do so from external sources? Further, after an uncertain start, they often become strongly engaged with their treatment. But, we may sometimes note, once treatment is established they make very slow progress, so that the therapy seems endless. The transference, which they establish, creates what I would like to call a "counter-transference depression" in which there is a feeling of wanting to help but with the gloomy sense that any effort is bound to fail. To illustrate these dilemmas, I shall now discuss a clinical example.

Clinical study

A twenty-one-year-old man was referred because he was said to be depressed. When he was very young his father had left, and was then demonized by the rest of his family, who were all female. He did not describe himself as depressed, but more as being worthless. Furthermore, he described a sense of feeling compelled to do the opposite of what others wished, which could be called perverse.

At the outset of treatment, he professed that he thought that the sessions would be rather pointless. "After all", he said, "what is the point of talking", in a discouraging manner reflecting and communicating his demoralization. At the time, I felt that this was an angry refusal of the psychoanalytic enterprise upon which we were embarking. But, as time went on, I came to see this as a very vivid communication of his despair and a warning that I would have to experience the very same despair if I tried to help him. It seemed that he warned me that any wishes I might have to help would be dashed and I would be left facing the same empty void that he saw before him, created by the absence of his father and his desire for him.

In the course of working with him, it became clear that a major method for him to communicate his difficulties was the pattern of his attendance, in that he would sometimes fail to attend sessions. As a result of these enactments, he was convinced that he was despised by his psychoanalyst. However, this transference message provided the clue to his difficulty and how to work with it. Forthright interpretation of his absence, or sporadic attendance patterns, as resulting from feeling identified with a despised object was initially in defiance of his common sense. Nevertheless, it enabled him to understand that the root of his feeling of being despicable was an identification with his departed father, who was despised by the remaining family but for whom he yearned. It seemed that he mourned his father but had no one with whom to mourn this loss because of the other family members' antagonism to his father. Eventually, he began to see that the purpose of the identification "with the lost object" could possibly be a defence against his sense of abandonment. In the broadest of summary, it seemed that, within the immediate family, this young man had become the "ghost" of his father, attracting the same antagonism as did the absent figure of his father.

In regard to this case, the central point I wish to make is that this young person's difficulties were communicated by the enactment of absence in the transference via the pattern of his attendance. It communicated absence and the sense of nothingness in the counter-transference that went with it. It seemed that this young man was in identification with an image that his mother and sister had of his father. All this was unconscious, and the expression of pointlessness of the whole therapeutic enterprise (his words—"what is the point of talking") was, I think, part of the identification with the family image of the father, who was seen as someone "you couldn't talk to" (because, of course, he was absent.) All this work took many months to do and could only be achieved by taking advantage of the temporal dimension of the psychoanalytic setting enabling the emergence, via repetition, of internal psychic defensive structures.

In summary, this young man had suffered the departure and absence of his father and had experienced difficulties in mourning because he was the only male in the remaining family. In the trans-ference, he unconsciously expected his absences from treatment to be condemned without reprieve, but his absenting himself from treatment was experienced by him as resulting from an impulse over which he had little or no control. Thus, he presented with a predicament to which he thought there was, and could be, no solu-tion. He felt he could not help doing what he did, but expected to be condemned for it. It is therefore easy to see how he came impli-citly saying "you can't help me". While we can see that this young man would naturally experience a reaction of depression to these circumstances, it is not so easy to see what tied him so firmly to his difficulties. The statement "you can't help me" suggested that he was unconsciously tied to the difficulties indissolubly, but then we have to wonder why he came at all. This is an example of the paradox I referred to earlier.

This gives rise to two specific observations, which need explanation.

1.   Some experience creates an experience of absence in the subject that is communicated in the transference in the form of a para-dox. In this case, the paradox is that the patient keeps coming to say to the therapist "what is the point of talking".

2.   Seemingly destructive enactments are evidence of some kind of defensive structure, against the experience of absence, to which the patient is indissolubly tied; otherwise one must ask why the patient comes for help when there is no external compulsion to so do.

It might be thought that the patient uses the treatment to evacuate, by projective identification duly experienced in the countertransference, the painful experience of being abandoned. But such a conception does not explain the effectiveness of the interpretation of his absence in terms of his identification with an absent father. If the conception were the case, the interpretation of his absence from the session being an identification with the lost object would be therapeutically inert. In the event, this was not so, because it laid the foundation for being able to mourn effectively his departed father.

Nothingness in the countertransference as evidence of "blank mourning"—the impact of decathexis. At this point, a theoretical model is needed to account for how someone might come to experience a sense of absence and then communicate this experience by being absent in the transference. Green (1986) has suggested that, in adults, there is a form of pathological mourning, which is a response to what he terms "psychic holes" in experience. He terms the response *"blank mourning"*, and this reflects an impression of blankness or emptiness in the patient's consciousness. He proposed that such a picture results when an individual's mother becomes depressed or, indeed, preoccupied in such way that she is perceived by the child to be distracted or unavailable to the child. Hence, this picture is not necessarily a reaction to an actual bereavement or loss in itself but to a situation in which the mother becomes chronically unavailable to the child. As Green puts it, the mother cares for the child, but "her heart is not in it".

An implication of this is that when the subject experiences this kind of deprivation a twofold problem is presented to them. On the one hand, there is loss of the alive, responsive, and available maternal object, and, on the other, the distortion to the ego caused by relating to an absent mother. The dead mother is the mother absent to the child because her mind is taken up by the preoccupation that persistently takes her mind away from the child. *The important feature is the effect of the "dead mother" on the child's experience of the mother. This effect is that the child is plunged prematurely into an Oedipal situation; or, in other words, the triangle created by whatever preoccupies the mother, and which causes her to decathect her child.*

In Green's view, the blankness results from a major *decathexis* of the child by the primary maternal object. This decathexis creates a "hole" in psychic space. In the child's experience, this could be described as moving from an experience of being something to the mother to one of being nothing. As a result of this loss, it is accompanied by a *narcissistic identification by the child* with the absent, distracted, or preoccupied mother which re-emerges in the transference situation and in the countertransference, as a picture of blankness and emptiness.

Green then suggests that the empty space is filled by a *recathected object*. This recathected object I propose instead to call a *virtual*[1] *object*. I call this object "virtual" because it seems to be a reflection of something within the patient. This is a term borrowed from optics in that the reflection of an object in a mirror is called a virtual object. *It is being continually being re-created out of the child's omnipotence*,[2] in Winnicott's (1960) sense of the word, and therefore reflects the means by which the trauma of loss comes under the child's ego-control and subject to secondary process.

The virtual object reflects the patient's understanding of the reasons for the object's absence resulting from the subjective experience of being decathected. Being created out of the child's omnipotence, the virtual object has an infinite quality, which, to my mind, is not quite conveyed by recathexis. The driving force behind the creation is the desire, implied by the nothingness of absence, which causes the virtual object to be continually re-created. Because it is created out of the child's omnipotence, we may think of the virtual object *as a form of transitional object.*

Describing the virtual object as a form of transitional object is to emphasize that such an object connects the subject's internal reality to external reality, in the manner described by Winnicott (1951). For this reason, it does not suffice to call it simply a transitional object and leave it at that. This is because it does not emphasize enough the concept that the virtual object is a reflection of the child's understanding of the reason for their primary object's absence as a result of their experience of being decathected by their primary object.

The recathected *or virtual object* leads to a distortion of the ego, because there is inevitably a narcissistic identification (Freud, 1917) with it. The consequence of this process will be that the patient will inevitably communicate their experience of the absence of their object by being, in some way, absent themselves. It is equated with the absent mother and is constructed out of the unconscious explanation for the mother's absence. It therefore becomes the hated part of the loved object, which forms the basis of the narcissistic identification. Thus, the "shadow" of the virtual object falls upon the subject's ego and is readily observed in the transference.

Green's recathected object, he feels, renders unconscious a desperately intense homosexuality. This, in both girls and boys, is a feminine homosexuality if it seeks a close identification to the passive, absent maternal figure, which is dead to the child. Thus, the oedipal triangle, referred to above, is re-created, but now in a defensive form, *because it binds the subject to the passive, absent maternal figure in a potentially timeless manner as a defence against the possibility of loss.* This attachment, of course, creates a closeness that is inseparable, which becomes a powerful resistance to analysis because of the reluctance to give up the absent dead mother. If she comes alive, the danger is that she will leave again. Thus, the patient is locked into their defensive system against loss because they have created something that will never leave them.

Using these ideas to think about the situation of the young man just described, let us begin with his belief that his psychoanalyst despised him for being absent. By this means, it could be thought that he showed that he had developed an identification to the despised absent father. He, being the only remaining male in the family, responded to his father's absence by becoming the "ghost" of the absent father. In a sense, we might wonder whether this was a case in which *the family, rather than just the mother, was dead to him as an individual because of the force of their projections.*

His identity could then have been distorted when his remaining family saw in him their image of the departed father. He readily absorbed these projections because of his own difficulties in mourning his father's absence. In the transference, therefore, he expected to be treated with contempt for being absent. He enacted being a contemptible figure, which could be said to be both his absent father and the protest against his father's absence. He enacted his virtual object by his absence from his analysis so that I was left groping at the nothingness of my patient's absence just as he groped at the nothingness of his father's absence.

I propose, therefore, that we can use Green's model of blank mourning if we think of the family being dead to him as an individual and his mode of mourning his absent father by narcissistic identification (Freud 1917e) complemented the distorted mourning of the other family members. This emerged in the transference through his absence and his belief that he was regarded with contempt. This suggests that we can use the concept of blank mourning in *any situation in which there is decathexis of the subject.* This can be, as we shall now see, where decathexis arises as a result of the actual absence of the mother. The purpose of relating this situation is to show the virtual object much more clearly. In the situation just described, the virtual object was revealed in the young man's narcissistic identification with the despised absent father.

Clinical vignette: patient two

Another young man, who was in treatment for several years, initially reported a crippling lack of confidence and fear when in the presence of other people and a sense that others in his family were false and contemptible. In this case, it was his mother who left the family rather than the father.

The dominant features of the transference situation in the therapy were the extreme sensitivity he felt about the ends of sessions and holiday breaks. In terms of content, he was much preoccupied with how he was going to become more confident in his relations with his friends, colleagues at work, his bosses, and girls. This had a despairing quality about it, and, for some time, he felt this would never improve. But, despite his feeling in consciousness of the futility of the exercise (you can't help me), he never missed a session.

At the end of sessions, he would look at me with an odd combination of fear and hatred and say "see you later" as he left with a slight air of contempt, which increased as his fear of this contempt seen in me, by projection, receded. At the beginning of treatment, this pattern seemed simply to reflect his resentment of the ending of the session. But as time went on, it became clearer that the combination of these feelings—hate, fear, and contempt—beautifully captured, in the one moment, the moment he had in his mind of his mother leaving his father, with whom he identified. This therefore communicated to me his virtual object in the form of his angry contemptuous mother leaving him in a state of fear and helplessness.

The meaning of this moment became increasingly clear as the therapeutic work progressed. Analysis of this pattern, as an identification with his rejecting virtual mother, paved the way for him to find and visit his actual mother again, whom he had not met for years. Up to this point, his perception of his mother in consciousness was that she was harsh and castrating. He discovered her not to be, in reality, the violent heartless bully of his fantasies, *but actually depressed herself.*

This was a profound shock to him because it upset all the fantasies he had built up to rationalize what had happened to him. This new actual mother did not fit the violent virtual mother who had left him and whom he felt sure hated him. He could now see that his fear of women arose from his hatred of women, and in particular his mother. Hence, we could create a hypothesis that this unconscious hatred, implied by his conscious fear, had then been the stuff out of which the virtual object of a hateful and hating mother had been created. His hatred had then to be projected and denied because acknowledgement of his own hate would entail assuming a guilt-ridden responsibility for the departure of his loved object.

The net effect had been to void him of his aggression, which led in turn to his lack of confidence and the belief that others looked upon him with contempt. However, this lack of confidence was the price exacted for avoiding a sense of his responsibility for his mother's departure. That is, his overriding need to maintain his mother as a good object transformed the hatred of his loved mother into an unconscious belief on his part that his hatred of his mother had driven her away. The consequence of this belief being unconscious was that he was in consciousness afraid of her, as he was of all women he desired. These defensive manoeuvres meant that his unconscious understanding was that his hate had driven his loving mother away, whereas his conscious understanding was that his hateful mother had left him.

We could see how, in the re-encounter with his actual mother, the terrifying virtual maternal object was thrown into sharp relief and differentiated from his actual mother. This virtual mother had been created in the space left by the departure of his actual mother. It had then powerfully determined his psychic life and the conscious experience of his life. When he could see that this virtual figure was a product of his own mind, but had been experienced and perceived as if it were a fact of external reality, there was a considerable reduction in his anxiety after an initial profound shock.

There was also a radical shift in his capacity to reflect on his own mind and a realization that he did not necessarily know what was in the mind of the (m)other. The minds of others were there to be discovered and did not need to be automatically thought of as frightening or contemptuous. Perhaps in confirmation of this hypothesis was the belief that developed in him that he needed to stay in contact with his mother to enable him to have a relationship with a girl. It was this that enabled him to replace the old hating mother with a present alive mother through whom he could create a relationship with a woman. The gradual repair of this relationship indeed enabled him to think of having a relationship with a girl, which he successfully achieved.

The presence of absent figures in the Oedipal triangle of blank mourning

Let us now examine further the peculiar triangular Oedipal situation in which there is an insistent presence as a result of absence, which was discussed earlier. In this second case, a situation was created by the actual absence of the mother. Her absence gave rise to a *preoccupying preoccupied* mother in the patient's mind, who was a figure created out of trying to account for the fact of her departure. This explanation was pieced together out of the fragments of affect left in the wake of her departure. I mentioned earlier how this young person seemed to experience the ends of sessions. If we consider this in the light of his fear of his object's contempt and the subjective certainty that he would be rejected without a thought, then I think we can see a distorted Oedipal triangle similar to that described by Green. This time, however, the virtual internal maternal object is not just lost in a preoccupation but, in fantasy, angrily and contemptuously turning away to another unknown figure. This was enacted in the typical behaviour observed at the end of many sessions. In the first case, the young man responds to his father's absence by identifying with the family virtual object created in the space left by the father's departure from the family.

Therefore, one point of this Oedipal triangle is taken by a virtual object created out of the individual's unconscious understanding of the reasons for the missing figure's absence. But, there is *no separate and alive* figure outside the control of the individual's omnipotence to mediate the relationship with the remaining figure and prevent the subject being caught inextricably in a dyadic enmeshing with the virtual object.

It is clear that individuals trapped in these distorted Oedipal triangles are in a very complex situation from which they cannot escape and to which they have no choice but to respond. In this case, the young man responds to his actual mother's absence by creating the maternal virtual object, which is angrily turning away and rejecting him. The narcissistic identification with the hated aspects of his loved maternal object means that it is not surprising to find such a person reporting a lack of confidence, reminiscent of a false self (Winnicott, 1960).

At the clinical level, the false self can appear quite convincing, particularly as the only sign that it is a false self is the reported "lack of confidence". But this is not necessarily a "compliant false self", although it may be, which is thought to arise from a premature *over-impingement* by the maternal object. We are clearly concerned here with *under-impingement* by an actual object that turns into an *over-impingement by a virtual object.* It combined the hostility of the subject and the absence of the object into the creation of the virtual hating mother. When this structure was revealed by the patient's encounter with his actual mother, it was not surprising that the experience was one of profound shock.

Virtual objects are initially experienced in the transference through the powerful effect of an uncanny sense of absence or of something missing and, in the countertransference, by a sense of pointlessness. I propose that it is by this means that nothingness as it exists in a patient is symbolized and communicated in the transference. The paradox of nothingness is that it is full of desire but it can appear that the subject communicating nothingness in the transference wants nothing. This gives rise to the paradox of the subject who says "you can't help me", while they continue to come. Ultimately, it seems that the paradox brought by the patients I have been discussing arises because they, as subjects, are cathecting objects that decathect them. I propose then that this decathexis will inevitably be experienced in the countertransference in a comparable manner—"you can't help me"—implying that the psychoanalyst is of no interest to the patient, thus conveying the experience of decathexis.

Notes

1. Lacan (1988) uses the notion of the virtual object in a discussion of Optics in his seminar entitled "The topic of the imaginary".
2. When I use the term *omnipotence* here, I use it in the sense that Winnicott had when he discussed the meaning of omnipotence as an experience essential in the steps that lead to the first experiences of "me" and "not me". I say this to differentiate my use of the term clearly from other senses of the term.

References

Freud, S. (1917e). Mourning and melancholia. *S.E.*, *14*.

Green, A. (1986). The dead mother. In: *On Private Madness*. London: Hogarth.

Lacan, J. (1988). The topic of the imaginary. In: J.-A. Miller (Ed.), J. Forrester (Trans.), *The Seminar of Jacques Lacan, Book 1 Freud's Papers on Technique 1953–54*. Cambridge: Cambridge University Press.

Winnicott, D. W. (1960). Ego distortion in terms of true and false self. In: D. W. Winnicott (1965) *Maturational Processes and the Facilitating Environment* (pp. 140–152). London: Karnac.

CHAPTER SEVEN

Observing patients' use of the psychoanalytic setting to communicate an experience of absence: the work of progressive triangulation

James Rose

If the analysis described above is correct, then it would seem that what has been observed is a process by which a patient's subjective experience of being decathected is communicated to the psychoanalyst by means of the patient's use of the psychoanalytic setting. This has been initially a quite unconscious use, as revealed by the change following interpretation. Moreover, the emergence of transitional phenomena in the form of virtual objects enable us to make some interesting links between a patient's subjective experience (or their psychic reality) and their behaviour in external reality, or enactments, which can readily be observed by the treating psychoanalyst. Such links are made possible by the functioning of the psychoanalytic setting and I shall propose that the essential component of the setting making this possible is *the temporal dimension.*

Green's (1986) description of the child who experiences chronic decathexis by a preoccupied mother helps us to imagine a particular kind of experience that we might describe as "being a nothing". Thus, the mother "cares for the child but her heart is not in it". The experience of being chronically decathected we can imagine therefore as being one in which we do not feel we matter to someone centrally important to us.

In the last chapter, I suggested that the paradoxical clinical pattern in which a patient persists in coming to see their psychoanalyst to tell them that they cannot help them should not necessarily be seen as being destructive, cruel, or perverse. However, it is indisputable that it often takes some time to make sense of this apparently paradoxical pattern and it is not without some narcissistic cost to the psychoanalyst that some insight into the situation is finally achieved. Furthermore, it may seem for a while that the patient is untreatable. The temptation for the treating psychoanalyst is to foreclose on the treatment prematurely. The result can be, if this happens, that the patient's experience of decathexis is repeated with possibly devastating consequences.

What we are dealing with here is the representation of experience that has been chronically impossible for the patient, leading them to be experienced as impossible by those around them. We can see that the experience of decathexis is communicated by the patient to those around them so it can be said that a process of symbolization occurs. The point of creating the concept of the virtual object and seeing it as a transitional phenomenon is to describe the process of the creation of a representational symbol and the meaning it has and seems to communicate to others. This virtual object, therefore, is indisputably a subjective phenomenon, but its effects on the subject's "objective" world of others are easy to observe but take time to understand properly from the subject's point of view. This takes us to questions about subjectivity and objectivity.

Psychoanalysis as a science of subjectivity

If psychoanalysis is thought of as a science of subjectivity, or, in other words, how we come to know our own minds, then with the word "science" comes the connotation of objectivity. There has been in recent years an ongoing debate about models of subjectivity in psychoanalysis. Comparatively recently, an edition of *Journal of the American Psychoanalytical Association* was given over to "controversial discussions" on this matter (e.g., Greenberg, 2001). This debate about subjectivity partly centres on the place of objectivity in the endeavour to know our own minds. This is because, since the philosophical "enlightenment" of the sixteenth and seventeenth centuries, objectivity has become the means of ensuring the reliability and validity of our descriptions of the external world. From the inception of psychoanalysis, the question of how similar standards can be applied to the exploration of the internal world has been posed but not satisfactorily answered. Such questions are of central importance because they permit examination of the theoretical underpinning of psychoanalytic practice. Adequate answers may provide better means of conceptualizing and operationalizing our practice.

Objectivity about subjectivity in psychoanalysis

In many ways, the debate about models of subjectivity begins with the question of whether it is possible to assert any claim for *objectivity about subjectivity* in psychoanalysis. This has been felt to be essential by some if psychoanalysis is to establish its validity in terms acceptable to philosophers of science and, by extension, natural scientists. In recent years, there has been an enormous response to this fundamental question, which is far too large to summarize here, save in the very broadest of outlines. One part of this debate was a series of papers in the *International Journal of the Psychoanalytical Association* concerning "What is a clinical fact?" As part of this debate, Gabbard (1997) suggested that being objective implies taking a third person view, but this creates a conundrum concerning how we can take a third person view of a first person phenomenon without losing something crucial. Is not the third person view of the psychoanalyst inevitably subjective in some way?

Cavell (1998) suggested that we might find a way out of this conundrum by allowing the entry of the notion of objective reality, which facilitates the development of a discourse between two subjects (analyst and analysand) about something. This was referred to as a triangulation, and it is this sense of triangulation to which I shall confine myself in later discussion. Triangulation should not here be equated with more familiar psychoanalytic notions of triangulation, e.g., Lebovici (1982). Rose (2000) suggested that a practical application of this idea could be that the psychoanalytic setting provided a part of the something about which discourse between patient and analyst could occur. The subjectivities of patient and analyst could thus find each other in relation to this third and could then take the opportunity to reflect on the experience of their interaction in *nachtraglichkeit*.

At this point, some definition of subjectivity must be proposed. As an initial approach to this we might take subjectivity to mean what has been called the "first person view" (Cavell, 1993). This is customary in psychoanalytic thinking. Thus, Freud (1915e) held that:

> In psychoanalysis there is no choice for us but to assert that mental processes are in themselves unconscious, and to liken the perception of them by means of consciousness to the perception of the external world by means of the sense organs. [p. 171]

And, further, that

> Just as Kant warned us not to overlook the fact that our perceptions are subjectively conditioned and must not be regarded as identical to what is perceived though unknowable, so psycho-analysis warns us not to equate perceptions by means of consciousness with the unconscious mental processes which are their object. Like the physical, the psychical is not necessarily in reality what it appears to be. [*ibid.*]

Cavell's (1993, 1998) epistemological analysis of the problem of how we can come to know our own minds, argues that, because an implicitly Cartesian notion of subjectivity underpins much psychoanalytic theoretical conceptualization, it is open to various kinds of attack in the form of charges of positivism (i.e., I know what is good for you) or suggestion (i.e., this is what you think, but you don't know it). Indeed, she could well argue that these occur because psychoanalysts often assume an internalist view of subjectivity without realizing the implications of so doing. Hence, although they would profess to abhor such technical errors, their unwitting use of such a theory of subjectivity forces them into a position in which they risk such criticism.

In Cavell's view, such a first-person view of subjectivity inevitably leads, following Descartes, to a global scepticism about the perceived material world and to appear to force us to choose between *naïve realism*, i.e., that the world is as we perceive it to be, or *idealism*, i.e., that the objects of our perception and thought are subjective entities of some kind. Objectivity clearly will seem to be compromised. Cavell (1993) suggests that it is only when we make an internalist Cartesian assumption about meaning (i.e., the first-person view) that we are forced into this choice. But, if subjectivity and meaning is not to be assumed to be the first-person view, then what else could it be?

Cavell's (1998) thoughts on triangulation between two minds in relation to external reality allow us to think about the development of subjectivity in a different way. Her thoughts seem similar to some infant researchers who distinguish between primary and secondary intersubjectivity (Trevarthan & Aitken, 2001). Thus, while Trevarthan observes that newborn children seem predisposed to relate by response to their mothers, there is a move on to *secondary intersubjectivity* at about nine months of age when the child initiates something in the apparent expectation that the other person has a mind. There is, therefore, an intention to relate rather than simply a capacity to relate and this can be observed. For example, the child takes note of something in its surroundings and points it out to his mother with the intention that she responds. If this capacity has not developed by eighteen months, it may be prognostic of autistic spectrum disorder. Cavell's position therefore seems to be supported by empirical findings in the related field of infant research.

But, the truly radical aspect of Cavell's view is that subjectivity and meaning should not be taken as confined to the first-person view. This is because interaction with another mind requires language, which implies, first, *that meaning and subjectivity cannot be confined to the first-person view*; and second, *that subjectivity grows from intersubjectivity and not the other way round*. Cavell (1993), being a philosopher, draws heavily on the work of Wittgenstein (1953) and Davidson (1984), but it must be said that these philosophical perspectives have had small impact on psychoanalysts. However, her thoughts clearly have a link with various French psychoanalytic theorists on subjectivity—notably Lacan and Raymond Cahn. She notes that she is in agreement with Lacan on two fundamental points: first, that language is a necessary condition for the unconscious, and second, that language is necessarily social.

It seems to me that these issues can be explored further through the examination of the clinical examples described in the previous chapter. The particular clinical phenomenon I would like to consider is that of an apparent absence in the transference. The patient seems to communicate a sense, by one means or another, that something is missing and that there is nothing that can be done about it. This can give rise, often mistakenly, to a perception of deficit in the patient by an assessing psychoanalyst or that the individual concerned is unsuitable for psychoanalytical treatment because of a learning difficulty.

The point of choosing this phenomenon is to use Cavell's (1998) idea that coming to know one's own mind requires discourse with another mind in relation to or about something. The question I propose is whether this formulation can be further examined if this something *seems* to be nothing. This may appear rather like a parlour game. Nevertheless, the purpose is serious for two reasons.

First, Cavell's model implies that the "something" is concretely external to both minds, which might lead some to query the practical relevance and use of this model to psychoanalysts who are concerned with internal phenomena. Absence and the associated sense of nothingness is indisputably a subjective experience internal to one of the minds in discourse. But we have also observed that this internal phenomenon has potentially serious consequences in the subject's "objective" social world. The virtual object thus embraces and forms a bridge between the subject's internal objects and their external ones to the point that its effects are hard to identify accurately and its causes hard to trace.

Second, if we can observe how something internal to a patient that starts as a meaningless experience or *nothing* but becomes something through some process of externalization that can be understood by both analyst and analysand, then I propose that we will have witnessed what Cavell (1993, p. 20) means by the "interpreter's perspective". This is how she looks at subjectivity in a different way from the purely internalist "first person view". The mind acquires a sense of meaning from its interpretations of the world and the means by which it has learned to do this is through discourse with significant others. In her words, "The strategy is to look at the process of interpretation to tell us not only how we know the minds of others but also how we are able 'to mean' ourselves".

To have a sense of being nothing in the countertransference is remarkable, because how can it be that we, as psychoanalysts, observe, and thereby relate to, nothing in a patient's mind? And yet, as a matter of fact, I think we clearly do, and comparatively often, because, as I said above, in assessment we will often be struck by a sense of something being absent, a deficit or a distortion of psychic processes by something that does not seem to be immediately apparent. It might be said to be a clear case in which "nothing noths".

Logically speaking, because it can never exist in itself, nothing has no meaning in itself. But, *in discourse with another mind over a period of time*, I hope I have shown above that it can acquire meaning, just as the maintenance of analytic neutrality allows the patient's desire for the analyst to be revealed. Furthermore, it seems to offer the possibility of understanding how the subjective experience of *nothing* (*or deficit*) can be seen transforming into a sense of *nothingness* because of the understanding of the emergence of the patient's (also known as the subject) *unconscious desire* in the psychoanalytic process. What was initially experienced as nothing becomes a sense of nothingness, if we can identify an implied desire.

This will inevitably take time and, it seems to me, it is the temporal dimension that holds the key to resolving the conundrum of trying to be objective about subjectivity. If we look at the emergence of the meaning that nothing acquires as it becomes nothingness—through the revelation of desire—within the psychoanalytic setting, I think we can see the functioning of the intersubjective learning system as it deals with a uniquely subjective phenomenon. In vernacular terms, we might say that we can observe the psychoanalytic process making something out of nothing.

The infinite nothingness of absence

When we say that someone is absent, the word "absent" can have a quantitative or a qualitative meaning. We can mean that they are not in a particular place in the physical and temporal sense or that they are not with us in the psychological sense. Absence is a deceptively complex idea; being equivalent to nothing, or, alternatively, a negative of something, or a quality in itself. Russell (1903) defined the logical zero of magnitude as the contradictory opposite of each magnitude of its kind, which implies that zero must imply something as well as mean nothing. We can assume, therefore, that absence describes something about an object in either logical or vernacular terms.

At this point, some might ask whether there is any point in thinking about the relationship of nothing to absence because the point of absence is precisely that it is the absence of something. In reply, I would say that those patients who are wrestling with the consequences of an absence often create an experience in the countertransference of helplessness, pointlessness, and emptiness, which reflects their own experience. An important aspect that should be noted at this point is the *infinite quality* of nothing, because within the class of nothing, the part is the same as the whole. In the terms of Matte-Blanco (1975), nothing is, therefore, an infinite set. Nothingness, therefore, can be thought of as an infinite experience (Rayner, 1981). This infinite quality leads more precisely to the qualitative experience of the nothing*ness* of absence, which stands in contrast to the quantitative nothing. If absence is a complex idea, the conceptual difficulties of nothingness are even greater. From the point of view of the theory of object relations it seems difficult to see how we relate to nothingness as an object, and yet it seems to me that in some way we must, because we do relate to absence. Logically, it is hard to grasp how we could be said to relate to nothing, and yet, as I hope to show, relating to nothingness can be observed.

The concept of nothingness is an idea that has been approached from an ontological point of view. Nothingness can be said to have *being* in spite of the impression that nothingness might be thought of as the *negative of being*. This creates the question of how we are, or can become, conscious of its being. Nothingness, to the existentialist point of view, has an implication for consciousness and therefore can be, following Brentano, as intentional as anything else in consciousness. One might say that a glass is full of nothingness and essentially mean the same as if we had said that the glass is empty and that there is nothing in it. But, the glass's being is such that it implies being full of something or having something in it, but the meaning of this, in turn, depends on the context. Hence, the meaning of the emptiness of an empty glass to a thirsty man in a desert is not perhaps the same as the emptiness of the desert and, therefore, has its own being. Sartre's (1943) analysis of nothingness through the description of going to meet Pierre at a café, only to find that he is not there, illustrates that *the qualitative experience of absence, or nothingness, is intimately bound up with desire*, because of the experience of lack.

Grunberger (1991) hints at this experience when he says; "During intra-uterine life . . . the self is omnipotent, in a state where space and time do not exist, since these result from the gap between the appearance of a need and its satisfaction" (p. 219). This suggests the possibility of an infinite void. This void is seen by Grunberger to be the gap between the experience of a need and its satisfaction. When this gap is subjectively very long, or perhaps infinite and eternal, then we can get a metaphorical glimpse of the infinite nothingness of absence. We may hypothesize that we will see nothingness in situations where the subject yearns for, but despairs of, the possibility of satisfaction. Absence, as a description of these patients' experience, is, I feel, too pallid (even though it may describe our countertransference). It is too discrete a notion precisely because of its connotation of something as opposed to the infinity of desire implied by Grunberger's gap between the appearance of a need and its satisfaction. Initially, however, absence may be all that we initially experience in the countertransference because of the efficacy of the defences against the subject's experience of infinite despair.

We could see in the examples in the previous chapter that this subjective experience is communicated to the psychoanalyst by an experience of the presence of absence in the transference.

In the clinical vignettes given so far, it will be clear that the enactments providing the experience of decathexis in the countertransference were in relation to the patient's use of the setting. The patterns, as a result, took some while to be identified because the underlying structure lay buried amid the to and fro of the ongoing analytic process. It is therefore worth giving an example of a situation of the experience of decathexis in the transference expressing itself in a more immediate and unmistakeable way. The situation occurred in the course of the treatment of a woman in her mid-thirties, who had entered treatment on account of a persistent insomnia that was psychiatrically diagnosed as depression.

Her problems seemed to derive from her being a replacement child for a loved "beautiful" boy, who had died in very early infancy. Being a girl, she felt that it seemed her mother had been unable to attach to her as a girl and throughout her childhood had related to her as if she were, in fact, the lost beloved boy, while at the same time berating her for not being the boy—a paradoxical experience. Her mother's pathological mourning, therefore, effectively meant that the patient was cathected by her mother as a boy but actively decathected as a girl. In response to this paradoxical situation, the patient had complied with her mother's wishes and trained in the occupation assigned to her by her mother, with the result that she felt that she had been forced into something that was not her. The abiding quality of her disturbance was that somehow she did not feel real.

The patient had entered treatment in her late twenties and became strongly attached to her analyst, who eventually had to terminate the treatment as he was leaving the country. Not surprisingly, this was very distressing for this patient, and her analyst suggested that she enter treatment with myself. This move was not at all easy for this patient, because she had found emotional attachment opened her to great anxiety. For quite a time she held her relationship to me at arm's length. However, after about eighteen months, it was clear that her attachment and trust in me was increasing as her anxieties receded in the light of the ongoing experience of the treatment. What was interesting was that she eventually saw that I was not simply a replacement for her preceding therapist, but that she could experience me as someone in my own right. Being thus faced with the emotional reality of her attachment to her analyst and its potential emotional consequences, she began to experience a return of her depression at the core of which was her dread of being decathected.

To illustrate this, in process terms, she arrived on a Friday to begin the session by announcing that she would have to miss the following Friday because she would be away. She was going to be pursuing an interest of which she told me her mother had disapproved. At this point, I simply made a silent mental note and acknowledged her announcement. She then continued to tell me about how unfairly treated she had been at work in that she felt her contribution had been overlooked and unacknowledged as if she did not exist. There was considerable bitterness in this narrative, and she felt that it had much to do with the depression that seemed to be hovering around her at weekends, which she found worrying. As she had been speaking, I had been struck by the fact she was telling me about being treated as if she did not exist but also that, in announcing that she was not going to be present in a week's time, she made no mention of a desire, or request, to find another time for us to meet. This was curious because it seemed to communicate both that I was being treated as if I did not exist and that she expected to be treated by me as if she did not exist. Could it be, I thought to myself, that she was in identification in these moments with a decathecting object as a defence against being decathected?

Accordingly, I intervened by taking up with her how she had told me of her pending absence and that what seemed to be missing was any thought that she might ask for replacement session. Perhaps, I interpreted, she feared to do this because, as she had become more attached to me, she dreaded making any such request for fear of being dismissed, which hid a certainty that she would be replaced. This thought clearly surprised her; she replied saying it had never occurred to her that she *could ask*.

I noted that she did not say simply that it never occurred to her to ask, which seemed to mean that, in the transference, the decathecting object was her analyst. The use of the words *"could ask"* implied that the power to ask was consciously experienced as lying outside her control. I therefore said that her reply strongly suggested that she was experiencing me as someone who would not tolerate any desire on her part to pursue her own interests and, at the same time, to miss her session. This surprised her even more, and she gratefully asked if we could move the session time.

This exchange seemed to make it clear that the returning feelings of depression was the consequence of her increased feelings of attachment to what she unconsciously dreaded would turn out to be another decathecting object. The emotional consequence for her of absenting herself from her analysis, however temporarily, seemed to be that she risked discovering an object indifferent to her. We could therefore see that, for her, the price of following her own desire was to risk abandonment. Perhaps her increasing confidence enabled her to take the risk that was essential to discovering whether her unconscious assumption about her object was true. In the event, the proposed change of time could not be achieved but it did n0t matter—the fact was that she had had a glimpse of an object willing to embrace the complexity of her feelings.

In the following session, she reported that she had experienced an extraordinary sense of freedom resulting from the realization that if her object could be experienced as embracing complexity, she too could have a mind capable of experiencing events at different levels. It reinforced a sense of feeling real. But the fact that the session time could not be changed meant that she had left the session feeling extremely angry.

This was because she felt that the replacement sessions I had offered her were impossible for her to accept. "You give with one hand, but take away with the other." But, having told me of her anger with me, she suddenly realized that she had omitted to tell me the whole period that she was going to be away. The alternative dates that I had offered her coincided with the dates she was going to be away. These she had omitted to tell me *but she had assumed I must know.*

When she realized, in the course of the session, that I could not possibly have known, she could see the effect of her aggression with the phantasied virtual object that she had placed in the psychic hole created by her absence from me. This absence implied that I was absenting myself from her, which in turn created a sense of my decathexis of her.

This short account is given as another example of a patient's unconscious use of the setting to communicate her experience of decathexis and its consequences for her understanding of her relationship to her own desires. It also shows her understanding of how she expected to be understood by her object. In this case, a virtual object, which is a decathecting object, is placed in the psychic hole in experience created by my expected decathexis of her resulting from her withdrawal from me.

It is also possible to see the despair resulting from the belief that her object would not tolerate any complex feeling, but simply demanded unquestioning devotion. As a result, her version of the clinical paradox experience referred to above was that she returned to keep telling me that she unconsciously felt that *I* wouldn't *help her.*

Temporality and progressive triangulation

It has been suggested (Rose, 2000) that the concept of triangulation proposed by Cavell (1998) as the process by which we can come to know our own minds enabled us to think about the function of the psychoanalytic setting in the treatment. Rose proposed that it could function as an aspect of objective reality, which the patient could use to communicate something important to their psychoanalyst about their psychic reality. It was proposed that the objective setting could offer a hook on to which features of a patient's internal world could reveal themselves; first as behaviour, then as experience that could in time acquire meaning.

This "objective reality", however, has to be taken in its broadest sense if it is to be of much use to the practising psychoanalyst. It must include perceptions and impressions of objects and affects of the most subjective and subtle kind because the most meaningful aspects of communication between patient and psychoanalyst concern psychic reality that will be expressed, enacted, and experienced partly through the medium of the setting.

By taking a sense of "something being missing" in the patient's experience and the psychoanalyst's countertransference experience of a deficit as being the feature permitting triangulation, we can see how a very internal subjective experience can be made manifest through the patient's "use" of the setting. I put "use" in quotes because it seems that the patient has little conscious intent or control over this use. The best we can say is that a patient unconsciously uses the setting to communicate his predicament in the only way he can. Perhaps to think of "use" as a reflection of the patient's unconscious response to the psychoanalytic situation will get closer to what happens.

In the two examples described in the preceding chapter, it can be seen that the painful experiences for which the two patients sought help were expressed by their unwitting use of the psychoanalytic setting to communicate their predicament to the analyst. Thus, my first patient could usefully be thought of as unconsciously telling me about the effect of his absent father by being absent himself. It might have been tempting to consider his absence as being an attack on his object. Perhaps, in consciousness, it was, but it seemed more effective in the treatment to see it as an unconscious communication about a narcissistic identification with an absent object. Similarly, the second young man could be thought of as showing me how he experienced his mother's departure in the manner that the session would finish. Again, it could have been seen as an expression of hatred towards the object for abandoning him. But it seemed more fruitful to view it as a communication of his experience of being left by a hating object.

By these means these two young men revealed the objects for which they yearned but felt, because they could never reach them, that they faced the nothingness of the void described by Grunberger. The patient just described communicated her predicament by showing the limitation on what it was possible for her to think, which revealed her virtual object to be one that avoided complexity. Such objects are initially obscure because recognizing the yearning for them causes great psychic pain. Further, the inevitable narcissistic identification with the object means that it will form part of the defensive system against loss. But, because of the repetitive and consistent nature of the psychoanalytic setting, these patterns, and the virtual objects that they imply, become recognizable and thus capable of analysis.

The purpose in this chapter of thinking about the phenomenon of absence in the transference and the countertransference is that it allows us to see the acquisition of meaning of this "nothing" as it becomes *nothingness*. This acquisition of meaning can be observed clearly because of the iterative aspect of the psychoanalytic setting. The sense of nothingness is achieved when the desire, reflected by the narcissistic identifications, is revealed. It seems to be the case that there can be no such thing as nothing in the patient's mind because the virtual object precludes it. Nothingness, with its implied desire, is the driving force behind the creation of virtual objects, which are formed—in *nachtraglichkeit* (or afterwardsness)— out of the affective fragments left by decathexis.

In the manner that these virtual objects reflect experience and desire, they are experienced in the transference. By this means, they become meaningful and capable of furnishing the means of communication and, potentially, understanding between the patient and their psychoanalyst, just as any other symbol can. It is this feature that, to my mind, contributes powerfully to the psychoanalytic endeavour being meaningful and conceivably possible because it emphasizes the learning process, which must take place over time. It is this that makes the psychoanalytic endeavour objective.

Subjectivity, objectivity, and temporality

Renik (1998) recently asserted in support of an intersubjectivist stance that the subjectivity of the psychoanalyst was irreducible. Hanly and Hanly (2001) and Loux and Pitman (2001) criticized this assertion about the *irreducible subjectivity* of the psychoanalyst. These examinations have sought to enquire into what we mean by *objectivity*. The Hanlys introduce a notion that they call critical realism. In their view, the analytic process requires the capacity, in both analysts and analysands, to entertain the possibility of being "corrected" by new evidence that has turned up in the analytic process. In the course of an analysis, patients will exert a great deal of pressure upon analysts to persuade them to see the world as they see it. In so doing, they will stir powerful feelings that will make it hard to think clearly or to maintain an open mind. This subjectivity, they argue, is not an epistemological subjectivity but a psychological one, springing from our human frailties. A psychological subjectivity, however, is not the same as an epistemological one, which avers that that there is no subject–object differentiation between patient and analyst and that the subjectivity of the psychoanalyst is, by definition, irreducible. When such a position becomes absolute, the implication seems to be that psychoanalysis as an enterprise becomes well-nigh impossible if it is intended to help a patient establish the truth of their psychic reality. The Hanlys feel that, when questions about what is subjective and what is objective in an analysis are not left to be settled by evidence, then an unhelpful confusion results from the absolutist claim of the psychoanalyst's irreducible subjectivity. In their words, "It is to this absolutism that critical realism objects" (Hanly & Hanly, 2001).

Louw and Pitman (2001) critique the position of Renik (1993, 1998) on the irreducibility of the psychoanalyst's subjectivity by saying first that he "appears to have set up a false dichotomy between his notion of subjectivity and a rather absolutist, transcendence notion of objectivity". They also object to Renik's position that, as they see it, had the implication that there could be no gain in the psychoanalyst's objectivity. This they felt was not established, because the psychoanalyst's perspective is clearly modified as he/she incorporated the different perspectives of the patient and those of his/her internal objects. If this change occurred, then the analyst's subjectivity cannot be irreducible. It is, perhaps, important to wonder at this point whether irreducible is here being understood as a *qualitative* concept or a *quantitative* one.

Louw and Pitman accepted that the psychoanalyst's subjectivity could never be eliminated as a quality, but this is not the same as being irreducible in the sense of being a quantity. Indeed, they suggested that Renik treated these two aspects as being equivalent. It is clear that in claiming that the analyst's subjectivity can be reduced in the quantitative sense, Loux and Pitman were, as were the Hanlys, placing the psychoanalytic endeavour firmly in its temporal context.

This, in itself, emphasizes the significance of the temporal dimension of the psychoanalytic process in *a process of progressive triangulation.* It may not seem very remarkable to think of a psychoanalysis as a learning system, but when we do so the temporal dimension is immediately emphasized.

As a result, if temporality is accepted, it then seems necessary to add the word progressive to triangulation, because the learning system implies a succession of related triangulations as the analysis proceeds. One could use the word "iterative" rather than progressive, but I prefer the latter because, as the learning system builds and develops as it goes through repeated iterations, the result of triangulation becomes progressively more complex. Patterns of these triangulations will emerge with the passage of time, progressively revealing and building a metaphorical structure of the patient's inner world as the transference unfolds. As we have observed in the cases described, the work of progressive triangulation indeed enables something to be made out of nothing. It seems to me that the emphatic inclusion of the temporal dimension enables psychoanalysts to approach a resolution of the conundrum of trying to be objective about subjectivity.

References

Cavell, M. (1993). *The Psychoanalytic Mind.* Cambridge, MA: Harvard University Press.

Cavell, M. (1998). Triangulation, one's own mind and objectivity. *International Journal of Psychoanalysis, 79*: 449–467.

Davidson, D. (1984). *Inquiries into Truth and Interpretation* Oxford: Clarendon.

Freud, S. (1915e). The unconscious. *S.E., 14*: 161–215. London: Hogarth.

Gabbard, G. (1997). A reconsideration of objectivity in the analyst. *International Journal of Psychoanalysis, 78*: 15–26.

Green, A. (1986). The dead mother. In: *On Private Madness*. London: Hogarth.

Greenberg, J. (2001). The analyst's participation: a new look. *Journal of the American Psychoanalytical Association, 49*(2): 359.

Grunberger, B. (1991). Narcissism and the analytic situation. In: Sandler, Person, & Fonagy (Eds.). *Freud's "On narcissism: an introduction"* (pp. 216–228). New Haven, CT: Yale University Press.

Hanly, C., & Hanly, M. A. F. (2001). Critical realism: distinguishing the psychological subjectivity of the analyst from epistemological subjectivism. *Journal of American Psychoanalytical Association, 49*(2): 515.

Lebovici, S. (1982). The origins and development of the Oedipus complex. *International Journal of Psychoanalysis, 63*: 201–215.

Loux, F., & Pitman, M. (2001). Irreducible subjectivity and interactionism: a critique. *International Journal of Psychoanalysis, 82*: 747.

Matte-Blanco, I. (1975). *The Unconscious as Infinite Sets*. London: Duckworth.

Rayner, E. (1981). Infinite experiences, affects and the characteristics of the unconscious. *International Journal of Psychoanalysis, 62*: 403.

Renik, O. (1993). Analytic interaction: conceptualizing technique in the light of the analyst's irreducible subjectivity. *Psychoanalytic Quarterly, 62*: 553–561.

Renik, O. (1998). The analyst's subjectivity and the analyst's objectivity. *International Journal of Psychoanalysis, 79*: 487.

Rose, J. S. (2000). Symbols and their function in managing the anxiety of change: an inter-subjective approach. *International Journal of Psychoanalysis, 81*.

Russell, B. (1903). *The Principles of Mathematics*. London: Routledge.

Sartre, J.-P. (1943). *Being and Nothingness: An Essay on Phenomenological Ontology*. H. E. Barnes (Trans.). Paris: Gallimard.

Trevarthan, C., & Aitken, K. (2001). Infant intersubjectivity: research, theory and clinical applications. *Journal of Child Psychology and Psychiatry Annual Research Review, 42*.

Wittgenstein, L. (1953). *Philosophical Investigations*. London: Blackwell.

CHAPTER EIGHT

Some conclusions

James Rose

T his book is intended to be a brief tour of the ways in which symbols have been thought about by psychoanalysts over the past century or so. We began with a brief statement by Freud. He reflects the state of psychoanalysis at the time he wrote the paper. It was struggling to establish itself in the early part of the twentieth century, and this partly meant substantiating the claim for a particular view of the unconscious. Perhaps Freud's boldest proposal was the idea that dreams were intelligible, but there were others, too, which can seem as extraordinary today as they seemed then. Not least of these was that the unconscious of one mind can be in communication with another unconscious. The creation of the psychoanalytic setting, and the adoption of a stance of free-floating attention by the psychoanalyst as he listened to the free associations of the patient, allowed a new perspective to emerge. By being out of the analysand's field of view, Freud placed himself in a position to listen to the unconscious of the analysand as it spoke to him.

The existence of symbols as subjective phenomena were then open to a new understanding by being brought under this new microscope. Dreams and their symbolism seemed particularly promising as "the royal road to the unconscious". But it transpired that there was no dream symbol lexicon, even though it was possible to see how the form of dream symbolism formed ways of understanding the process of the development of the transference in the consulting room. However, symbols were interesting for what they signified was repressed. In Jones (1916), only what was repressed needed to be symbolized. Thus, it was the content of what was repressed that was represented by a symbol, as Joan Riviere's tennis playing patient demonstrated (see Introduction).

In the next phase of development, which coincided with development of the metapsychology of psychoanalysis, it began to be thought that the form and structure of symbols reflected the mental functioning of the patient and could be used to deepen understanding of a patient's intrapsychic functioning. There is no doubt that this makes much sense and is very useful in assessing a patient's capacities and how to work with them creatively and intelligibly. Thus, the nature of a symbol reflected an analysand's capacity for mental functioning. In Segal's (1957) view, the symbolic equation reflected functioning in the mode of the paranoid–schizoid position and the symbolic representation reflected functioning in the mode of the depressive position. This was an acute clinical observation that had valuable clinical application.

Then, as psychoanalysis began to think about broadening its scope of application, conceptions of the symbol as a representative of the repressed or of mental functioning were supplemented by the idea of the symbol as the *symbolon—an object cut in two, constituting a sign of recognition when those who carry it (them) can assemble the two pieces.* A debate on the expanding scope of psychoanalysis that took place in 1975 at the IPA congress in London was entitled "On changes in psychoanalytic practice and experience: theoretical, technical and social implications". In one of contributing papers, André Green used the notion of *symbolon* to think about *the function of the analytic setting and its relation to mental functioning as shown by the process of symbolization.*

In one of his conclusions to his paper, he draws attention to the effort in the psychoanalytic session, through attention given to the analytic setting and to mental functioning, to create the conditions necessary for the formation of the analytic object through symbolization, by taking into account the intervention of the third element, which is the setting, in the dual relationship.

This idea takes psychoanalysis into a quite new epistemological direction and new vistas and perspectives open themselves. We could say that symbolization was expanded from being evidence of repression and mental function; that is, what it represented to its, some might say, original function, which was to communicate. When a symbol is seen to emerge in the psychoanalytic discourse between analyst and analysand in the context of the psychoanalytic setting, then we can observe its communicative function in the fullest sense. I have sought, in my contributions to this book, to demonstrate this feature by discussing the symbolization of nothingness. I have used this because it is indisputably both a subjective phenomenon and difficult to represent except through enactment and the transformation of negative hallucinations into virtual objects and other transitional phenomena.

However, to do this involves something of a shift in one's epistemological stance in terms of how one thinks about subjectivity and objectivity. Marcia Cavell's conception of triangulation set out in her reprinted in this volume helps us to do this because she shows us how discourse with another mind about something external enables us to come to know our own mind. When we place this alongside Green's ideas, we can start to see the process by which an individual, faced with the inevitable anxiety created by not knowing the future, will seek to represent and then communicate these anxieties to another mind. The psychoanalytic setting is a unique creation in which to observe representation being created and then communicated. The process by which this occurs can be called progressive triangulation. It harnesses the iterative feature of the psychoanalytic process and the compulsive repetition, which drives it.

We arrive at the conclusion that how a symbol, as a subjective phenomenon, is conceived in psychoanalysis has expanded as it has developed philosophically and epistemologically. We have come to think of the symbol not just as a representative of the repressed but also, as the Botellas (2005) have demonstrated, as evidence of a function which enables the unrepresentable to be represented and communicated—hence the title of this book.

References

Botella, C., & Botella, S. (2005). *The Work of Psychic Figurability*. Hove: Brunner-Routledge.

Jones, E. (1916). The theory of symbolism. In: E. Jones (Ed.), *Papers on Psycho-Analysis*. London: Maresfield Reprints.

Segal, H. (1957). Notes on symbol formation. *International Journal of Psychoanalysis, 38*: 391–397.

BIBLIOGRAPHY BY SUBJECT

Symbols as evidence for the unconscious

Freud, S. (1916c). A connection between a symbol and a symptom. *S.E.*, *14*: 339–340. London: Hogarth.

Jones, E. (1916). The theory of symbolism. In: *Papers on Psycho-Analysis*. London: Maresfield Reprints.

Riviere, J. (1924). Phallic symbolism. *International Journal of Psychoanalysis*, *5*: 85.

Symbolization is the basis of all the talents: relating to the world

Klein, M. (1930). The importance of symbol-formation in the development of the ego. *International Journal of Psychoanalysis*, *11*: 24–39.

Segal, H. (1957). Notes on symbol formation. *International Journal of Psychoanalysis*, *38*: 391–397.

Art creates nature: inner and outer

Milner, M. (1952. Aspects of symbolism in comprehension of the not-self. *International Journal of Psychoanalysis*, *33*: 181–194.

Winnicott, D. W. (1951). Transitional objects and transitional phenomena. In: *From Paediatrics to Psychoanalysis*. London: Hogarth, 1982.

Symbols and communication: relating to others

Cavell, M. (1998). Triangulation, one's own mind and objectivity. *International Journal of Psychoanalysis, 79*: 449.
Fink, B. (2005). Lacanian clinical practice. *Psychoanalytic Review, 92*(4).
Rose, J. S. (2000). Symbols and their function in managing the anxiety of change: an inter-subjective approach. *International Journal of Psychoanalysis, 81.*

Psychic figurability: representing the unrepresentable

Rose, J. S. Making something out of nothing: observing the work of progressive triangulation in understanding the presence of absence in the transference.

INDEX